"I dare you to page through Lucie's book and not feel a flutter of joy. These are desserts to make you dream."

—**DORIE GREENSPAN**, James Beard Award–winning author of *Dorie's Anytime Cakes*

"I can't wait to gift Lucie's cookbook to all my friends and family . . . and then come over to eat their versions of her magically delicious recipes sprinkled with flowers."

—**ANNASOPHIA ROBB**, actress

"Best cakes! Clearly made with love and care. Delicious and GORGEOUS! Almost too beautiful to eat."

—**MAGGIE GYLLENHAAL**, filmmaker

"In *Cake From Lucie*, the beloved baker shares not only her recipes but also her story: one of flavor, flowers, and finding her way from France to New York."

—**KERRY DIAMOND**, founder of Cherry Bombe

Cake From Lucie

CAKE
FROM LUCIE

Recipes and Techniques from the French Countryside to New York City

LUCIE FRANC DE FERRIERE

with Lauren Salkeld
Photographs by Lucia Bell-Epstein
Illustrations by Maya Netzer

CLARKSON POTTER/PUBLISHERS
NEW YORK

CHOCOLATE
PRODUIT EN FRANCE
EARL Gibert

To my mother, my lifelong inspiration.

Contents

155 DESSERT

WHIMSICAL TAKES ON CLASSIC DESSERTS

199 GOÛTER

THE FRENCH TRADITION OF A 4 P.M. TREAT

Lucie

FROM LUCIE.
263

INTRODUCTION

As I sit down to write this, my kettle is boiling, a generous slice of cake rests on my plate—a portion some might say could serve two—and my dog, Dalida, is fast asleep. It sounds like the perfect, cozy afternoon, but it's 11 p.m. on a Tuesday, after a long day at the bakery. My approach to baking mirrors my approach to life. People have called my baking whimsical, and I love that. Whimsy implies something imperfect, messy, and full of personality—just like me. I embrace it because, truth be told, I'm not an organized person, but I am a generous one. I love the look of overflowing cream and jam on a cake, preferring to see it oozing from a slice rather than tucked away neatly. For me, flavor always comes first, and design follows naturally.

I grew up in the countryside of southwest France, in a small village called Pessac-sur-Dordogne, with our family vineyard, Château Carbonneau, as my playground. My mother ran a bed and breakfast with a tearoom. My father made wine and raised cows, dogs, cats, and chickens, whose eggs made the most wonderful cakes! In a town of just four hundred people, teenage curiosity pushed me to explore beyond our quiet hills. I studied art history in Toulouse, then in Rome, and ultimately completed my master's degree in Leeds in northern England. After graduating, I landed an internship at an art gallery in Manhattan, packed my bags, and within two weeks, arrived wide-eyed with no clue how the subway worked. I was jet-lagged and five minutes late on my first day, but I kept repeating to myself: "Fake it until you make it."

My bakery, From Lucie, was born out of both necessity and love. In April of 2020, after three years in New York, I lost my gallery job at the height of the pandemic. Flights home felt impossible, and I was madly in love with my then boyfriend (now husband), Gurpreet, so I decided to stay in New York. Gurpreet had just opened Sunday to Sunday, a cafe on the Lower East Side, and when their pastry suppliers closed, I started baking for them in my free time. At first, it was just simple things like cookies and banana bread, but cakes have always been my true love and what I really wanted to devote my time to. There wasn't a market for layer cakes at the cafe, so when pop-ups gained traction around the city, I started working with different brands to sell my cakes. That led me to embrace social media. I didn't have a storefront, and it was a way for people to discover and buy my cakes. It was also a great way to share my baking journey and stay connected with friends and family back home during a troubling time.

Over the next three years, my cake business grew dramatically, and I realized I needed my own space. We opened the tiniest bakery in a charming spot in the East Village that I found almost by accident. Despite its moldy floors and clutter, I saw its potential as a welcoming place where people could pick up a cake or stop in for a slice and a coffee. We crowdfunded the renovation (thank you to our 475 backers), bringing touches of my home country to the bakery, from the mustard yellow exterior inspired by houses found in the South of France to the ceramic tiles we used for our address that came from my uncle in Menton. On our opening day, January 14, 2023, I watched in awe as a line started wrapping around the block. We were completely unprepared, but with the help of some friends and family, we served nearly everyone. That day, I felt overwhelming gratitude for the community we had built.

This book is for anyone who doesn't know where to start with baking. As much as I'd love to say I was born baking, that's not the case. I was born eating my mother's incredible desserts, but did I bake a lot? No. I simply watched her. It wasn't until I moved to New York that I truly learned to bake—spending hours on the phone with my mum, scouring the internet, flipping through cookbooks, and mostly trying and failing, and trying and failing again, until something finally clicked. I once handed out samples of a chocolate chip cookie I was working on at Gurpreet's cafe, and a customer said, "Oh, I didn't know you sold rocks here." Instead of giving up, I took the feedback and perfected the recipe, which the *New York Times* declared "the classic" on their list of five stellar cookies in New York City.

I must credit my parents for my persistence. My mother, an English teacher, left everything behind in New Zealand to follow my father back to his home in France. Her teaching degree didn't transfer internationally, so with little money and an inherited, timeworn home, my parents set out to build a life together from scratch. My dad, with no formal training, planted vines with a dream of making wine, while my mum saw the potential in our house. She took on countless jobs—teaching piano, sewing children's clothes for the local market, among others—just to buy wallpaper and paint, and transformed the house room by room. She made curtains and cushions from fabric she could barely afford, eventually turning our home into a bed and breakfast. She dug and planted her own garden, and in the kitchen, she worked her magic with meals and desserts she learned from friends, family, or simply on the fly.

My parents taught me that if you pour your heart into something, people will naturally gravitate toward it. It won't be perfect—perfection isn't the goal—but it will be honest, fulfilling, and true to oneself. I'm grateful my family instilled in me the courage to take risks, embrace failure, and live without the weight of "what if." I'm equally grateful for what New York has given me. The city celebrates differences and innovation like nowhere else. When I started making cakes adorned with flowers, people said, "That's different—let me try it." The city fosters dreamers, pushing them to go beyond their limits. I'll never take that for granted.

My kind of baking is inspired by my childhood on the farm. Working with seasonal and fresh ingredients is at the core of my baking philosophy. I also focus on creating desserts that aren't overly sweet. It's not a critique, but American desserts (especially ones with buttercream) tend to be a bit too sweet for me. My approach to baking is to balance flavors, so if a cake is on the sweeter side, the buttercream will offer a tangy, refreshing contrast.

Flowers and herbs are the heart of my baking. When I was growing up, the bed and breakfast entertained guests from around the world. There was always something baking in the oven, and the house was filled with the scent of fresh cakes and flowers from the garden. That combination of smells is where my inspiration for using florals and herbs in my baking began.

When it comes to decorating, I never plan too much in advance, as I enjoy letting my creativity flow naturally, and I suggest you try the same. In this book, I hope to guide you in discovering your own style by sharing the flowers I love and use on my cakes, as well as the ways I decorate. I encourage you to experiment and find a style that works for you.

Throughout the book, you'll find "How to" sections that are meant to be moments where we can connect. They're a place where I can share insights I've learned through many rounds of trial and error—from the countless hours spent on the phone with my mum, asking why my cakes didn't turn out right, to combing through secondhand cookbooks to working with the talented bakers at my bakery, without whom I would be nowhere today. I'll show you how to make Swiss meringue buttercream exactly how I like it, how I choose flowers for decoration, and much more, while sharing the common mistakes to avoid.

This book isn't about perfection; it's about the joy of baking. I want to guide you through the same journey I took—from hesitation to confidence. Some recipes are effortless, made from ingredients you likely already have at home, while others are more intricate showstoppers. Either way, you'll find that there's always room for creativity.

I hope this book encourages you to embrace baking in a way that feels accessible and enjoyable. Let's start somewhere together.

263
RETAIL / RESTAURANT
FOR LEASE

EURS.
TIPS

Coldline
COMMERCIAL REFRIGERATION

INGREDIENTS AND TOOLS

I've always worried about being an "all the gear and no idea" kind of person, so I make it a point to work with what I have at home and buy only what is truly necessary. This isn't a list of every ingredient and gadget under the sun, but rather the ones I constantly rely on and think are worth highlighting.

INGREDIENTS

BROWN SUGAR: I use both light and dark brown sugar in my recipes. They are mostly interchangeable, but dark brown sugar will add a deeper flavor. Make sure you seal brown sugar well, as it will get hard and become unusable if you don't. You need to keep the air out, so the sugar stays moist.

BUTTER: I use unsalted (except for in my Salted Caramel, page 121) and ideally European.

BUTTERMILK: This should be cultured and pasteurized; low-fat is fine. If you don't have any at home, add 1 tablespoon lemon juice or vinegar (distilled white or apple cider) to every 1 cup (240ml) of whole milk.

CHOCOLATE: Chocolate might be my favorite thing to eat, so I am very particular about it. When it matters to the recipe, I call for a specific percentage of cacao, but otherwise, just be sure to use high-quality dark chocolate. The same goes for milk and white chocolate—use the highest quality, as it will have more depth and that will make a huge difference. When melting chocolate, always use bars or fèves, and avoid chips. Like a lot of French people, I think Valrhona is the best for baking.

CITRUS ZEST: This should be freshly and finely grated on a Microplane.

COCOA POWDER: I always use unsweetened Dutch-process cocoa powder, as it's less acidic, has a smoother, richer flavor, and is darker in color than natural cocoa powder.

CREAM CHEESE: Use only the ones that come in blocks and are not already whipped, as they will provide more structure.

EARL GREY TEA: Seek out a high-quality tea for the best flavor. If you plan to decorate with the leaves, make sure your Earl Grey tea contains some dried blue cornflowers.

EGGS: Always large. I prefer to use free-range eggs for better flavor and structure, and I always bake with room temperature eggs.

ELDERFLOWER SYRUP: Many syrups are made for cocktails and contain alcohol. For baking, it's important to use a nonalcoholic syrup to achieve the best flavor. I love the one made by 1883 Maison Routin.

FLOUR: I always use all-purpose flour and sift it at least once, but if I'm making a butter-based cake and have the time, I sift the flour three times. This refines it to create a more delicate crumb—it comes closer to baking with cake flour without the extra expense.

FLOWERS: I share a lot more about flowers in How to Decorate Cakes (page 83), but they must be organic, pesticide-free, and preferably edible. Keep them in a vase of water in the fridge so they last longer.

FREEZE-DRIED FRUIT AND DEHYDRATED FRUIT: Freeze-dried fruit should be crispy and crunchy, while dehydrated fruit should be soft and sweet. Dehydrated fruit can easily be made at home (see How to Dehydrate and Sugar Fruit, page 103), but I always buy freeze-dried fruit, as it requires special equipment and packaging to maintain its texture. My favorite are freeze-dried raspberries, as they add a lot of color for decorating—you'll see them on a lot of my cakes.

FROMAGE FRAIS AND MASCARPONE: Look for ones that are creamy and soft but firm enough to hold their shape.

GLUTEN-FREE FLOUR: Any all-purpose mix works, but make sure to use one that contains xanthan gum. I like Cup4Cup.

HEAVY CREAM (HEAVY WHIPPING CREAM): It must contain 35% or more milk fat. Anything less or reduced fat doesn't work (see How to Make Whipped Cream, page 223).

HERBS: I always use fresh herbs, except for dried culinary lavender. Don't try substituting with dried herbs; they won't have the same flavor.

INSTANT COFFEE AND ESPRESSO: I'm not a coffee drinker myself, but I know that if you want the coffee flavor to be more prominent in your cakes and buttercreams, use instant espresso, and if you want a more subtle flavor, use instant coffee.

MILK: Always whole milk.

PLANT-BASED BUTTER: I recommend using a plant-based butter that mimics the texture of regular butter—it should be solid when cold but able to soften to creamy for baking. Earth Balance is the closest I've found, and Miyoko's comes next.

PLANT-BASED MILK: Soy milk is my preference because it has the highest protein and fat content, so it holds its structure better and helps cakes brown nicely. Almond milk is an okay substitute, but oat milk doesn't work.

SALT: At the bakery, we use fine kosher salt, but fine sea salt works, too (just make sure your salt isn't iodized). It's important to use fine salt, so it enhances the flavor without adding texture to a sponge or buttercream. I occasionally finish desserts with flaky Maldon sea salt.

TAHINI: You want tahini that's rich, smooth, and velvety. Always give it a good stir before measuring so it has a pourable paste-like texture.

VANILLA BEANS, EXTRACT, AND PASTE: When I'm making a vanilla whipped cream or vanilla buttercream, I always use vanilla bean paste or fresh vanilla seeds scraped from the pods. I avoid using extract in those instances, because it doesn't deliver as much vanilla flavor, and you don't get those lovely dark flecks. However, when vanilla is being used only to enhance the other flavors in a recipe, such as for my brown butter maple buttercream (used on my Pear Raspberry Brown Butter Maple Sheet Cake, page 111), extract works just fine.

YOGURT: I always use whole-milk plain yogurt, not Greek.

TOOLS

BAKING SHEETS: I use both quarter baking sheets (9 × 13-inch / 23 × 33cm) and half baking sheets (13 × 18-inch / 33 × 45cm). Make sure they have a 1-inch (2.5cm) rim around the edge.

BISCUIT CUTTERS: I recommend getting a set of biscuit cutters so you have a range of sizes—depending on the set, you may even be able to use them for my Rose Raspberry Sandwich Biscuits (page 211).

CAKE TURNTABLE: Any turntable will do, but a metal one on the sturdier side is best.

CARDBOARD CAKE ROUNDS (AND SQUARES): If you're using a cake board to present your cake, you can have fun with different colors and shapes, but I do love a classic white one so the cake can really shine. Make sure the cardboard is greaseproof to avoid any buttercream stains.

DIGITAL SCALE: This is a necessary tool in baking for more precision.

DIGITAL THERMOMETER: An instant-read thermometer is always good to have on hand, and especially when making Swiss meringue buttercreams, jams, and curds.

INSULATED CAKE PAN STRIPS: These help cakes to bake more evenly, but if you don't want to invest in them, I have a trick. Fold a long strip of wet paper towels and wrap them in aluminum foil, then wrap that strip around the outside of your cake pan to insulate it.

METAL BENCH SCRAPER (ICING SMOOTHER): I do love a metal bench scraper, as it stays rigid, allowing you to be more precise, but if you already own a plastic scraper, it will work, too.

OVEN THERMOMETER: This is the most important tool for ensuring that your oven is at the right temperature. Try testing different areas in your oven to see if the temperature is uniform throughout or if there are any hot spots.

PARCHMENT PAPER: Essential for lining almost every baking pan in my recipes. If you bake a lot, consider investing in parchment sheets or rounds already cut to the size of your pans. They are a lifesaver!

PIPING BAGS: I use reusable piping bags made of coated canvas, but plastic ones are also fine.

ROLLING PIN: I use my grandmother's wooden one, and it does wonders. However, if you're on holiday somewhere and don't have one, just flour a glass bottle and use it as your rolling pin.

RUBBER SPATULA: Essential for getting all of the batter out of bowls.

SMALL OFFSET SPATULA: I use one of these for decorating but also for serving cake slices. It's multifunctional and indispensable.

STAND MIXER: This is your best friend. Hand mixers can do the job, but I highly recommend investing in a stand mixer, as it's more powerful and will free up your hands.

ZESTER: For finely grated zest, a classic Microplane is the best option.

130
OPEN
1 cup
237 ml

SIMPLE
Effortless Cakes for Every Day

LEMON HIBISCUS MINI CAKES

MAKES EIGHT 3-INCH / 7.5CM TWO-LAYER MINI CAKES

These spongy, moist lemon cakes have a perfect hit of zest and pair with almost any buttercream, but I particularly love the brightness of lemon combined with the floral notes of hibiscus. You can also use hibiscus to give the buttercream a beautiful natural pink color and can control how dark or light it is by how much you use. Many hibiscus powders are a bit brown, so for the most vibrant color be sure to use one that's bright pink.

A crucial tip for the cakes is to make sure all of the ingredients are at room temperature. Also, when adding the dry ingredients, whisk them in by hand—it helps maintain the air in the batter and ensures everything is properly combined. For the buttercream, don't be tempted to skip the 10-minute beating process. It's essential for incorporating air, bringing the buttercream together beautifully, and achieving that lovely, glossy finish.

LEMON MINI CAKES

- Canola oil spray or canola oil, for the pans
- 1¾ cups / 245g all-purpose flour
- 2½ teaspoons baking powder
- ½ teaspoon fine sea salt
- 1 stick plus 4 tablespoons / 168g unsalted butter, at room temperature
- ¼ cup / 60ml canola oil
- 1¼ cups plus 2 tablespoons / 275g granulated sugar
- 3 tablespoons grated lemon zest (from 3 medium lemons)
- 4 large eggs, at room temperature
- ¾ cup plus 2 tablespoons / 210ml buttermilk, at room temperature
- ¼ cup / 60ml freshly squeezed lemon juice (from 2 medium lemons)

HIBISCUS BUTTERCREAM

- 1½ teaspoons loose hibiscus tea leaves
- ¼ cup / 60ml boiling water
- 2 cups / 240g powdered sugar, sifted
- 2 sticks / 226g unsalted butter, at room temperature and cut into small pieces
- ⅓ cup / 80ml heavy cream
- 2 teaspoons hibiscus powder
- 1 teaspoon vanilla extract
- ¼ teaspoon fine sea salt

ASSEMBLY

- Small flowers and greenery (see page 88), for decorating
- Dehydrated fruit slices (page 103), crushed pistachios (page 83), and crushed freeze-dried raspberries (page 83), for decorating (optional)

1. **FOR THE LEMON MINI CAKES:** Set a rack in the middle of the oven and preheat to 350°F / 180°C. Spray or brush the sides of eight 3-inch / 7.5cm round mini cake pans with canola oil, then line the bottoms with parchment paper.

2. Sift the flour and baking powder into a medium bowl. Add the salt.

3. In a stand mixer fitted with the paddle, beat the butter on medium-high speed until creamy, about 1 minute. Add the canola oil, granulated sugar, and lemon zest and beat until light and fluffy, about 2 minutes. Scrape down the bottom and sides of the bowl, then add the eggs, one at a time, and beat on medium speed, scraping the bowl before each addition and again at the end, until fully incorporated. Add the buttermilk and lemon juice and beat until fully incorporated, about 30 seconds. The batter may appear slightly curdled—this is normal.

4. Remove the bowl from the stand mixer, then gradually add the flour mixture, gently folding it in with a whisk just until there are no streaks. Do not overmix!

5. Divide the batter evenly among the prepared pans. Tap the pans on the counter to even out the batter, then arrange on a baking sheet.

6. Bake until a skewer inserted into the center comes out clean, 20 to 25 minutes.

7. Let the cakes cool in the pans on a wire rack for 30 minutes. Jiggle the pans upside down to release the cakes. Remove the parchment paper. Flip the cakes right-side up on the rack to cool completely.

8. **FOR THE HIBISCUS BUTTERCREAM:** In a small bowl, combine the hibiscus tea leaves and the boiling water and let steep until completely cool.

9. In a stand mixer fitted with the paddle, add 3 tablespoons of the tea (discard the tea leaves and any extra brewed tea). Add the powdered sugar, butter, heavy cream, hibiscus powder, vanilla, and salt and mix on low speed just until combined, about 30 seconds. Increase to high speed and beat, scraping the bowl as needed, until light, fluffy, and slightly shiny, about 10 minutes. Mix on low speed for 1 to 2 minutes more to remove any air bubbles and make the buttercream easier to pipe.

10. **TO ASSEMBLE:** If any mini cakes have domed tops, once they are completely cool, use a serrated knife to slice off the domes, so the cakes are flat and even. Carefully cut each cake horizontally in half to create two layers. Place the cake bottoms, flat-sides down, on a cake board or serving plate.

11. Put about 1 cup / 200g of the buttercream into a piping bag fitted with a plain round tip with a ½-inch / 13mm or similar diameter. Holding the pastry tip about 1 inch / 2.5cm above a cake bottom and starting from the edge, pipe a rounded ring of buttercream around the perimeter. Pipe a dollop of buttercream in the center, then use a small offset spatula to gently spread the dollop so it covers the top of the cake, while leaving the buttercream ring intact. Repeat with the remaining cake bottoms.

12. Carefully place the cake tops, flat-sides up, on top, then gently wiggle them into the buttercream. Add more buttercream to the piping bag as needed. Repeat the above process to frost the tops of the mini cakes.

13. Arrange a small flower and some greenery (see Tips for Working with Flowers, page 85) on each cake. Add a slice of dehydrated fruit and sprinkle the crushed pistachios and freeze-dried raspberries on the buttercream, if desired. The mini cakes (without foliage) keep covered in the refrigerator for up to 3 days. Remove the cakes about 2 hours before serving, so the buttercream has time to soften.

VANILLA CAKE

MAKES ONE 8-INCH / 20CM TWO-LAYER CAKE

We all have that one friend who only ever wants vanilla cake for their birthday—and honestly, sometimes that's exactly what hits the spot. This recipe is all about the vanilla bean paste, so treat yourself to a good one. I've been using the Heilala brand from New Zealand, and it's done miracles for my baking. When you're beating the eggs and sugar for the cake, be sure to get plenty of aeration, as it's the key to creating the cake's soft and fluffy texture. Once the batter is ready, bake it right away—letting it sit will cause it to deflate. You can easily swap the square cake pans for round ones and add as many hundreds and thousands (sprinkles) as you like. The more the merrier!

VANILLA BEAN CAKE

Canola oil spray or canola oil, for the pans
1¼ cups / 175g all-purpose flour
3 tablespoons cornstarch
1 tablespoon baking powder
8 large eggs, at room temperature
1½ cups plus 2 tablespoons / 330g granulated sugar
1 tablespoon vanilla bean paste
¼ teaspoon fine sea salt
2 tablespoons whole-milk yogurt (not Greek), at room temperature
4 tablespoons plus 2 teaspoons / 65g unsalted butter
1½ teaspoons canola oil

VANILLA ITALIAN BUTTERCREAM

Distilled white vinegar
140g egg whites (about 4 large), at room temperature
¼ teaspoon cream of tartar
¼ teaspoon fine sea salt
1⅓ cups / 265g granulated sugar
4 sticks / 452g unsalted butter, at room temperature and cut into small pieces
1 teaspoon vanilla bean paste

RASPBERRY GLAZE

2½ cups / 300g powdered sugar, sifted, plus more as needed
⅓ cup / 80ml freshly squeezed lemon juice (from 2 medium lemons)
½ teaspoon ground freeze-dried raspberries or freeze-dried raspberry powder

ASSEMBLY

Hundreds and thousands (sprinkles), for decorating

1. FOR THE VANILLA BEAN CAKE: Set a rack in the middle of the oven and preheat to 350°F / 180°C. Spray or brush the sides of two 8-inch / 20cm square cake pans with canola oil, then line the bottoms with parchment paper.

2. Sift the flour, cornstarch, and baking powder into a medium bowl.

3. In a stand mixer fitted with the whisk, whip the eggs on medium speed for 30 seconds to combine. Add the granulated sugar, vanilla bean paste, and salt and whip on high speed until pale, thick, and fluffy, 7 to 8 minutes.

4. Remove the bowl from the stand mixer, then add the yogurt and use a whisk to gently incorporate it without deflating the egg mixture. Add the flour mixture in two batches and gently fold with a rubber spatula just until there are no streaks. Do not overmix!

5. In a small saucepan, melt the butter over medium heat and bring to a boil. Remove from the heat and carefully pour the hot butter into the batter, followed by the canola oil, and gently fold just until incorporated.

6. Divide the batter evenly between the prepared pans, smoothing the tops.

7. Bake until the cakes are golden brown and the tops spring back when lightly pressed, about 30 minutes. A skewer inserted in the center of each cake should come out clean or with just a few moist crumbs.

8. Let the cakes cool in the pans on a wire rack for 15 minutes. Flip the cakes onto the racks, then remove

RECIPE CONTINUES

the parchment. Leave the cakes upside down and let cool completely.

9. FOR THE VANILLA ITALIAN BUTTERCREAM: Use a paper towel and about ¼ teaspoon of white vinegar to wipe all over the surface of a large heatproof bowl and the bowl of a stand mixer.

10. In the clean bowl of a stand mixer fitted with the whisk, whip the egg whites, cream of tartar, and salt on high speed for about 20 seconds to combine. On high speed, gradually add ⅓ cup / 65g of the granulated sugar and whip until soft peaks form, about 1 minute.

11. In a small saucepan, combine the remaining 1 cup / 200g granulated sugar and ⅓ cup / 80ml water and stir over low heat until the sugar is fully dissolved and the mixture is completely clear. Increase the heat to medium and cook, stirring constantly, until the mixture registers 240°F / 115°C on an instant-read thermometer. At this point, the egg white mixture should be at soft peak.

12. With the mixer on high speed, slowly and carefully pour the hot sugar into the mixer bowl, aiming for the spot where the bowl curves inward, so the hot sugar doesn't slide down the bowl or hit the whisk attachment and splash. The hot sugar cooks the egg whites, giving the meringue its structure. The stand mixer bowl will become warm. Continue whipping until the bowl cools almost to room temperature (about 70°F / 21°C). The meringue should be silky and white and have soft peaks with some structure.

13. Scrape down the bottom and sides of the bowl, then swap the whisk attachment for the paddle. On medium-high speed, gradually add the butter, one piece at a time. The meringue will look a bit soupy at first, but it will come back together and start to hold its shape. Once all the butter is added, continue beating until the buttercream has a fluffy, silky, cloud-like texture. Scrape the bowl, then add the vanilla bean paste and beat on high speed for 30 seconds.

14. FOR THE RASPBERRY GLAZE: Sift the powdered sugar into the bowl of a stand mixer, then add the lemon juice and ground freeze-dried raspberries. Using the whisk attachment, whip on low speed until just combined, then increase the speed to high and whip until thick and smooth, 1 to 2 minutes.

15. TO ASSEMBLE: Place a cake layer, flat-side down, on a cake plate or stand.

16. Put the buttercream into a piping bag fitted with a plain round tip with a ½-inch / 13mm or similar diameter. Holding the pastry tip about 1 inch / 2.5cm above the cake and starting about ¼ inch / 6mm from the edge, pipe a rounded ring of buttercream around the perimeter, then pipe zigzags of buttercream in the middle of the cake so it's completely covered. Using a small offset spatula, gently spread the buttercream zigzags to fill in any gaps and connect them to the outer ring of buttercream, while leaving it intact. You can use all the buttercream here or reserve a bit for decorating (see How to Assemble, Frost, and Cut a Layer Cake, page 53).

17. Carefully place the second cake layer, flat-side up, on top, then gently wiggle it into the buttercream.

18. Slowly pour the raspberry glaze onto the cake, using a small offset spatula to gently spread it to the edges to fully cover the top. Sprinkle with hundreds and thousands! The cake is best the day it's assembled, but it keeps covered in the refrigerator for up to 1 day. Remove the cake about 2 hours before serving, so the buttercream has time to soften.

CHOCOLATE STOUT ROSEMARY CAKE

MAKES ONE 8-INCH / 20CM CAKE

This recipe is from my mother, and it's the first cake I baked when I started my baking journey in New York City. It's also a bestseller at her tearoom back in France, so I had to snag it. To put my own spin on the buttercream I infuse it with rosemary—I love the richness of the chocolate and stout paired with the herb's woodiness. Using stout can be intimidating and strange at first, but it adds moistness to the cake and enhances its chocolate flavor. Fromage frais is France's cream cheese and is slightly lighter than the American counterpart. If you can't find it, feel free to substitute regular cream cheese, as long as you beat it for slightly longer to incorporate a bit more air.

CHOCOLATE STOUT CAKE

Canola oil spray or canola oil, for the pan
1¾ cups / 245g all-purpose flour
1¾ teaspoons baking soda
½ cup / 120g sour cream, at room temperature
2 large eggs, at room temperature
1 tablespoon vanilla extract
¾ cup / 180ml Irish stout, such as Guinness
1 stick plus 6 tablespoons / 198g unsalted butter, at room temperature and cut into small pieces
1½ cups plus 1 tablespoon / 315g granulated sugar
¾ cup / 60g unsweetened Dutch-process cocoa powder, sifted, plus more (optional) for dusting

ROSEMARY FROMAGE FRAIS BUTTERCREAM

¼ cup / 55g Rosemary-Infused Butter (recipe follows), at room temperature and cut into small pieces
2 tablespoons unsalted butter, at room temperature and cut into small pieces
1½ cups plus 3 tablespoons / 200g powdered sugar, sifted
1⅓ cups / 300g fromage frais or cream cheese, at room temperature and cut into small pieces
⅛ teaspoon fine sea salt

1. FOR THE CHOCOLATE STOUT CAKE: Set a rack in the middle of the oven and preheat to 350°F / 180°C. Spray or brush the sides of an 8-inch / 20cm round cake pan with canola oil, then line the bottom with parchment paper.

2. Sift the flour and baking soda into a medium bowl.

3. In another medium bowl, whisk together the sour cream, eggs, and vanilla.

4. In a large saucepan, combine the stout and butter and warm over medium heat until the butter is completely melted. Remove from the heat, then whisk in the granulated sugar and cocoa powder until fully incorporated. Add to the sour cream mixture and whisk until fully incorporated. The batter should be dark in color and very thin. Whisk in the flour mixture just until there are no clumps of flour. Pour the cake batter into the prepared pan, smoothing the top.

5. Bake until the cake springs back when lightly pressed and a skewer inserted in the center comes out clean, 50 minutes to 1 hour.

6. Let the cake cool in the pan on a wire rack for 30 minutes. Carefully run a small offset spatula between the edges of the pan and the cake, then flip the pan onto the rack and tap it to make sure the cake is released. Remove the parchment paper. Use a second rack or a plate to flip the cake so it's right-side up on the rack. Let cool completely.

7. FOR THE ROSEMARY FROMAGE FRAIS BUTTERCREAM: In a stand mixer fitted with the paddle, beat the rosemary-infused butter and unsalted butter on medium-high

RECIPE CONTINUES

speed until lighter in color and slightly voluminous, about 2 minutes. Scrape down the bottom and sides of the bowl, then add half of the powdered sugar and beat on medium-low speed until mostly incorporated. Scrape the bowl again, then add the remaining powdered sugar and beat on medium-low speed until fully incorporated—the mixture will be quite firm. Scrape the bowl, then add the fromage frais in four batches, beating on medium speed and scraping the bowl before each addition, until smooth and uniform. Add the salt and beat on high speed until very fluffy, about 1 minute. The buttercream will be very soft. Cover and refrigerate for at least 1 hour to firm up the buttercream and give it more structure.

8. Place the cake flat-side down on a cake plate or stand. Using a rubber spatula, put a large dollop of the buttercream on top of the cake. Use a small offset spatula to spread the buttercream on top of the cake, then use the tip of the spatula to create some swooshes and texture on top. Dust with cocoa powder, if desired. The cake keeps covered in the refrigerator for up to 3 days. Remove the cake 1 to 2 hours before serving, so the buttercream has time to soften.

Rosemary-Infused Butter

MAKES ⅔ CUP / 150G

1 stick plus 4 tablespoons / 168g unsalted butter
¼ cup / 6g fresh rosemary needles, roughly chopped

1. In a small saucepan, melt the butter over medium-low heat. Remove from the heat, stir in the rosemary, cover, and let stand for 30 minutes (see How to Infuse Butter, page 39).

2. Pour through a fine-mesh sieve set over a medium bowl, pressing on the rosemary to extract as much flavor as possible (discard the rosemary). Cover and refrigerate, stirring every 20 minutes, until the butter starts to firm up, about 1 hour, then leave it alone to chill completely, for at least 1 hour and up to 1 week. The butter can also be well wrapped and frozen for up to 2 months; thaw in the refrigerator overnight.

How to
INFUSE BUTTER

I first started infusing butter when I wanted to work with herbs and florals in my cakes and buttercreams. A lot of recipes use extracts, but I find those make the flavor too intense and artificial. Other recipes use flavored syrups, which I think add too much sweetness. By infusing butter, which has a neutral flavor, with the actual herb or floral, it brings out its essence naturally. I'm using culinary lavender here, but you can infuse butter with almost any herb or floral you like. You can use infused butter to flavor any buttercreams or cakes, or simply add a touch of salt and enjoy it on toast—all the recipes make more infused butter than you will need, so there will be leftovers to enjoy. It elevates any baked good or dish with very little effort.

1. Measure the dried culinary lavender and the unsalted butter and cut the butter into small pieces.

2. In a small saucepan, melt the butter over medium-low heat.

3. Once the butter is melted, remove from the heat and stir in the lavender, making sure it's coated in butter and not just sitting on top.

4. Cover the saucepan and let the butter infuse for 30 minutes at room temperature.

5. Pour through a fine-mesh sieve set over a medium bowl, using a rubber spatula to press out all the butter and extract as much flavor as possible (discard the lavender).

6. Cover and place it in the refrigerator for 20 minutes.

7. Stir the butter—it will still be very liquid-y. Repeat this process every 20 minutes until the butter starts to firm up, about 1 hour total. The butter will still be soft, but it should be homogenous in consistency.

8. Press plastic wrap directly onto the surface of the butter, then return it to the refrigerator to chill until it has the consistency of regular refrigerated butter, at least 1 hour. Once the butter is firm, you can wrap it in parchment paper and secure it with ribbon or twine for gifting!

9. Bring the infused butter to cool room temperature before using it to make buttercream. It can also be wrapped in plastic wrap and refrigerated for up to 1 week or wrapped in a double layer of plastic wrap and frozen for up to 2 months; thaw it in the refrigerator overnight.

GLUTEN-FREE ZUCCHINI HONEY MASCARPONE CAKE

MAKES ONE 8-INCH / 20CM CAKE

When I was growing up, our vegetable garden produced so much zucchini that there were weeks when it felt like it was all we ate! Zucchini contains quite a bit of water, but I don't squeeze out any of it, as it creates an incredibly moist cake. The mascarpone buttercream is silky smooth and light, while a drizzle of caramelized honey lends the perfect note of sweetness. When I'm home in France, I always get honey from Dominique, a man in our village. He produces the best honey I've ever tasted. Use the extra caramelized honey as a topping for ice cream or to sweeten coffee, tea, or even hot chocolate (Chocolat Chaud, page 241).

ZUCCHINI HONEY CAKE

Canola oil spray or canola oil, for the pan
7 ounces / 200g zucchini (about 1 medium zucchini), ends trimmed
1 cup / 140g all-purpose gluten-free flour
1 teaspoon baking soda
¼ teaspoon fine sea salt
½ cup plus 2 tablespoons / 125g granulated sugar
½ cup plus 2 tablespoons / 125g (packed) light brown sugar
¾ cup / 180ml canola oil
3 large eggs, at room temperature
1½ teaspoons honey
1 teaspoon vanilla extract

CARAMELIZED HONEY

½ cup / 120ml honey

MASCARPONE BUTTERCREAM

2 cups / 455g mascarpone, cold
3 tablespoons crème fraîche, cold
3 tablespoons powdered sugar, sifted

ASSEMBLY

Crushed pistachios (page 83)
Small chamomile flowers with stems

1. FOR THE ZUCCHINI HONEY CAKE: Set a rack in the middle of the oven and preheat to 350°F / 180°C. Spray or brush the sides of an 8-inch / 20cm round cake pan with canola oil, then line the bottom with parchment paper.

2. In a food processor (or using the large holes of a box grater), shred the zucchini into thin strips. Measure 1½ cups / 175g of shredded zucchini and reserve the rest for another use. Do not press out any of the moisture from the zucchini.

3. Sift the flour and baking soda into a medium bowl. Add the salt.

4. In a stand mixer fitted with the paddle, mix the granulated sugar and brown sugar on low speed until combined, about 30 seconds. On medium-low speed, gradually add the canola oil, then continue beating until it's fully incorporated and the mixture looks like wet sand, about 1 minute. Scrape down the bottom and sides of the bowl, then add the eggs, one at a time, and beat on medium speed, scraping the bowl before each addition and again at the end, until fully incorporated. Add the honey and vanilla and beat on medium-high speed until incorporated, about 30 seconds. Scrape the bowl. Add the flour mixture in two batches and mix on low speed, scraping the bowl before each addition, just until there are no streaks. Do not overmix!

5. Remove the bowl from the stand mixer, then fold in the shredded zucchini with a rubber spatula just until fully incorporated. Pour the batter into the prepared pan, smoothing the top.

6. Bake for 25 minutes, then quickly rotate the pan, and continue baking until the cake is dark golden on top and springs back when lightly pressed, about 25 minutes more.

RECIPE CONTINUES

7. Let the cake cool in the pan on a wire rack for 30 minutes. Carefully run a small offset spatula between the edges of the pan and the cake, then flip the pan onto the rack and tap it to make sure the cake is released. Remove the parchment paper. Use a second rack or a plate to flip the cake so it's right-side up on the rack. Let cool completely.

8. FOR THE CARAMELIZED HONEY: In a small saucepan, warm the honey over medium-low heat, stirring occasionally—it will bubble and get darker—until it's amber in color and smells nutty, about 8 minutes. It should register 250°F / 120°C on an instant-read thermometer. Remove from the heat and let cool for 5 minutes. Stir the honey briefly and set aside to cool and thicken while you make the buttercream.

9. FOR THE MASCARPONE BUTTERCREAM: Add the mascarpone to a stand mixer, leaving behind any liquid in the container. Add the crème fraîche and powdered sugar and use the whisk attachment to whip on low speed until fully combined, about 30 seconds. Scrape the bowl, then whip on medium-high speed until the buttercream is thick and creamy and starts to make a slapping sound in the bowl, about 1 minute.

10. TO ASSEMBLE: If the cake is domed on top, once it's completely cool, using a serrated knife and starting about 1 inch / 2.5cm in from the edge, carefully trim the top to make it flat.

11. Place the cake, flat-side down, on a cake plate or stand. Using a rubber spatula, put about two-thirds of the buttercream on top of the cake. Use a small offset spatula to spread the buttercream into a thick, even layer on top of the cake, making it as smooth as possible.

12. Fill a piping bag fitted with a small to medium-size V-shaped Saint Honoré tip with the remaining buttercream. Starting in the center of the cake, pipe eight zigzags out to the edges of the cake, arranging them so there will be one zigzag on each slice of cake. Use a small spoon to drizzle some caramelized honey over the top of the cake, then sprinkle with the pistachios. Gently press the stem of a chamomile flower on the outside end of each zigzag. Enjoy right away, cutting the slices so there is a flower and a zigzag on each slice. The cake (without flowers) keeps covered in the refrigerator for up to 5 days. Remove the cake about 1 hour before serving, so the buttercream has time to soften.

GÂTEAU AU CHOCOLAT

MAKES ONE 10-INCH / 25CM CAKE

This is the perfect cake to make when you're having a bad day and want to treat yourself, and it just so happens to be gluten-free. Some might call it the French version of a brownie, but the whipped egg whites bring a lot of air that makes it far lighter and fluffier. When you put your fork in for that first bite, you can actually hear the bubbling, crackling sound of the egg whites. I like to eat this cake warm and drizzled with cold rose crème anglaise.

Softened unsalted butter, for the pan
14 ounces / 400g dark chocolate, preferably 64% cacao, roughly chopped
2 sticks / 226g unsalted butter, cut into small pieces
Distilled white vinegar
8 large eggs, separated and at room temperature
2 large egg yolks, at room temperature
1½ cups / 300g sugar
½ teaspoon fine sea salt
Rose Crème Anglaise (page 170), cold, for serving

1. Set a rack in the middle of the oven and preheat to 350°F / 180°C. Grease the sides of a 10-inch / 25cm round cake pan with butter, then line the bottom with parchment paper.

2. Fill a medium saucepan with about 1 inch / 2.5cm of water and bring to a simmer over medium-low heat. In a large heatproof bowl, combine the chocolate and butter, then set the bowl over the pan of simmering water, making sure the water does not touch the bottom of the bowl. Heat the mixture, stirring occasionally, until melted. Remove the bowl from the pan (careful—it will be warm!) and use a clean kitchen towel to carefully wipe any condensation from the bottom of the bowl. Let cool slightly.

3. Use a paper towel and about ¼ teaspoon of white vinegar to wipe the inside of a stand mixer bowl, making sure there aren't any traces of liquid or fat.

4. In the clean bowl of a stand mixer fitted with the whisk, whip the egg whites on medium speed until foamy, about 30 seconds. Gradually increase the speed to high and whip until stiff peaks form, about 3 minutes. Transfer the whipped egg whites to a large clean bowl.

5. Add the 10 egg yolks and the sugar to the stand mixer (you don't have to clean the bowl) and use the whisk to beat on medium-high speed until pale and doubled in volume, about 3 minutes. Scrape down the bottom and sides of the bowl. On low speed, gradually add the melted chocolate and butter. Scrape the bowl, then continue mixing just until there are no streaks, about 1 minute. Add the salt and mix briefly to incorporate it.

6. Remove the bowl from the stand mixer, then add about one-quarter of the whipped egg whites and gently fold with a rubber spatula to lighten the chocolate mixture. Add the rest of the whipped egg whites and gently fold just until there are no streaks and the batter is an even color. Pour the batter into the prepared pan, smoothing the top.

7. Bake until there is a crack on top of the cake and it feels firm to the touch—it may still be soft in the middle—about 45 minutes.

8. Let the cake cool in the pan on a wire rack for 30 minutes. Carefully run a small offset spatula between the edges of the pan and the cake, then flip the pan onto the rack and tap it to make sure the cake is released. Remove the parchment paper. Use a second rack or a plate to flip the cake so it's right-side up.

9. While the cake is still warm, cut it into slices and serve with the cold rose crème anglaise. The cake keeps covered in the refrigerator for up to 3 days. Warm it in the oven or microwave before serving.

BROWN SUGAR BANANA GOAT CHEESE BLACK PEPPER CAKE

MAKES ONE 8-INCH / 20CM CAKE

The natural sweetness of ripe bananas shines through in this moist and light cake, while brown sugar adds warmth and rich caramelized notes. But what really sets this cake apart is the tangy, creamy goat cheese buttercream that gets an unexpected but delightful kick from black pepper. Perfect for those who love a twist on traditional desserts, this cake is ideal for special occasions, afternoon tea, or just a quick treat.

BROWN SUGAR BANANA CAKE

Canola oil spray or canola oil, for the pan
2 very ripe bananas
½ teaspoon freshly squeezed lemon juice (from 1 medium lemon)
1¼ cups / 175g all-purpose flour
¾ teaspoon baking soda
¼ teaspoon fine sea salt
5 tablespoons / 75g unsalted butter, at room temperature and cut into small pieces
½ cup / 100g granulated sugar
¼ cup / 50g (packed) light brown sugar
2 large eggs, at room temperature
½ teaspoon vanilla extract
¾ cup / 180ml buttermilk, at room temperature
⅓ cup / 60g semisweet chocolate chips (optional)

GOAT CHEESE BLACK PEPPER BUTTERCREAM

1 stick / 113g unsalted butter, at room temperature and cut into small pieces
2½ cups / 300g powdered sugar, sifted
1 cup / 250g goat cheese, at room temperature
¾ cup plus 2 tablespoons / 195g cream cheese, at room temperature and cut into small pieces
¼ teaspoon freshly ground black pepper
⅛ teaspoon fine sea salt

ASSEMBLY

Whole fresh cherries with stems, for decorating

1. FOR THE BROWN SUGAR BANANA CAKE: Set a rack in the middle of the oven and preheat to 300°F / 150°C. Spray or brush the sides of an 8-inch / 20cm square cake pan with canola oil, then line the bottom with parchment paper.

2. In a small bowl, use your hands, a potato masher, or a fork to mash the bananas, making sure there are some small chunks remaining. Stir in the lemon juice.

3. Sift the flour and baking soda into a medium bowl. Add the salt.

4. In a stand mixer fitted with the paddle, beat the butter on high speed for 1 minute. Scrape down the bottom and sides of the bowl, then add the granulated sugar and brown sugar and beat on medium-high speed, scraping the bowl as needed, until fully combined and creamy, about 2 minutes. Scrape the bowl, then add the eggs, one at a time, and beat on medium speed, scraping the bowl before each addition and again at the end, until fully incorporated. Add the vanilla and beat until incorporated, about 30 seconds. On low speed, add the flour mixture in three batches, alternating with the buttermilk in two batches and scraping the bowl before each addition. Mix just until there are no streaks. Do not overmix! Add the banana mixture and mix just until incorporated.

5. Remove the bowl from the stand mixer, then gently fold in the chocolate chips (if using) with a rubber spatula. Spread the batter in the prepared pan, smoothing the top.

6. Bake until the cake springs back when lightly pressed and a skewer inserted in the center comes out clean, 45 to 50 minutes.

RECIPE CONTINUES

7. Let the cake cool in the pan on a wire rack for 15 minutes. Carefully run a small offset spatula between the edges of the pan and the cake, then flip the pan onto the rack and tap it to make sure the cake is released. Remove the parchment paper. Leave the cake upside down and let cool completely.

8. FOR THE GOAT CHEESE BLACK PEPPER BUTTERCREAM: In a stand mixer fitted with the paddle, beat the butter on medium-high speed, scraping the bowl as needed, until lighter in color and slightly more voluminous, about 3 minutes. Scrape the bowl, then add the powdered sugar in two batches and beat on medium-low speed, scraping the bowl as needed, until fully incorporated, about 3 minutes total. On medium-high speed, gradually add the goat cheese, followed by the cream cheese and beat, scraping the bowl as needed, until fully incorporated, about 3 minutes total. Beat on high speed for 30 seconds, then add the pepper and salt and beat on medium speed just until incorporated, about 15 seconds. The buttercream will be creamy and airy.

9. TO ASSEMBLE: Place the cake, flat-side down, on a cake plate or stand. Using a rubber spatula, put a large dollop of the buttercream on top of the cake. Use a small offset spatula to spread the buttercream on top of the cake, then use the tip of the spatula to create some swooshes and texture on top of the cake. Finish the cake with a few cherries. The cake keeps covered in the refrigerator for up to 5 days. Remove the cake about 1 hour before serving, so the buttercream has time to soften.

CARROT FROMAGE FRAIS CAKE

MAKES ONE 8-INCH / 20CM TWO-LAYER CAKE

This cake just might be our second-best seller at the bakery, right after our Salted Dark Chocolate Chip Cookies (page 203). It's moist and light, with delicate notes of cinnamon, and the fromage frais buttercream—fromage frais is French cream cheese—brings a touch of tanginess that perfectly complements the carrot cake. If you can't find fromage frais, feel free to substitute cream cheese, as long as you beat it for slightly longer to add a bit more air. This is a great recipe for swapping in gluten-free flour. Just be sure to use an all-purpose blend that contains xanthan gum. My favorite thing about this cake is that it becomes even more moist and complex in flavor the longer it sits in the fridge. Thank me later!

CARROT CAKE

Canola oil spray or canola oil, for the pans
14 ounces / 400g carrots (about 6 medium carrots), peeled and trimmed
2 cups / 280g all-purpose flour
2 teaspoons baking soda
¼ teaspoon ground cinnamon
⅛ teaspoon fine sea salt
1 cup / 200g granulated sugar
1 cup / 200g (packed) light brown sugar
1⅓ cups / 320ml canola oil
5 large eggs, at room temperature
1 teaspoon vanilla extract

FROMAGE FRAIS BUTTERCREAM

1 stick / 113g unsalted butter, at room temperature and cut into small pieces
2¼ cups / 270g powdered sugar, sifted
2 cups / 450g fromage frais or cream cheese, at room temperature and cut into small pieces
Pinch of fine sea salt

ASSEMBLY

Large and small flowers and greenery (see page 88), for decorating
Dehydrated fruit slices (page 103), crushed pistachios (page 83), and crushed freeze-dried raspberries (page 83), for decorating (optional)

1. FOR THE CARROT CAKE: Set a rack in the middle of the oven and preheat to 350°F / 180°C. Spray or brush the sides of two 8-inch / 20cm round cake pans with canola oil, then line the bottoms with parchment paper.

2. In a food processor (or using the large holes of a box grater), shred the carrots into thin strips. Measure out 2½ cups / 250g of the shredded carrots and reserve the rest for another use.

3. Sift the flour, baking soda, and cinnamon into a medium bowl. Add the salt.

4. In a stand mixer fitted with the paddle, mix the granulated sugar and brown sugar on low speed until combined, about 30 seconds. On medium-low speed, gradually add the canola oil, then continue beating until it's fully incorporated and the mixture looks like wet sand, about 1 minute. Scrape down the bottom and sides of the bowl, then add the eggs, one at a time, and beat on medium speed, scraping the bowl before each addition and again at the end, until fully incorporated. Add the vanilla and beat until incorporated, about 30 seconds. Add the flour mixture in three batches and mix on low speed, scraping the bowl before each addition, just until there are no streaks. Do not overmix!

5. Remove the bowl from the stand mixer, then fold in the shredded carrots with a rubber spatula just until fully incorporated.

6. Divide the batter evenly between the prepared pans, smoothing the tops. Bake for 30 minutes, then quickly rotate the pans and continue baking until the cakes are dark golden on top and spring back when lightly pressed, 25 to 30 minutes more.

RECIPE CONTINUES

7. Let the cakes cool in the pans on a wire rack for 30 minutes. Carefully run a small offset spatula between the edges of the pans and the cakes, then flip the pans onto the rack and tap them to make sure the cakes are released. Remove the parchment paper. Use a second rack or a plate to flip the cakes so they are right-side up on the rack. Let cool completely.

8. **FOR THE FROMAGE FRAIS BUTTERCREAM:** In a stand mixer fitted with the paddle, beat the butter on medium-high speed until lighter in color and slightly more voluminous, about 3 minutes. Scrape the bowl, then add the powdered sugar in two batches and beat on medium-low speed, scraping the bowl as needed, until fully incorporated, about 3 minutes total. Scrape the bowl, then add the fromage frais in four batches and beat on medium speed, scraping the bowl before each addition and again at the end, until smooth and uniform. Add the salt and beat on high speed until very fluffy, about 1 minute. The buttercream will be very soft. Cover and refrigerate for at least 1 hour to firm it up and give it more structure.

9. **TO ASSEMBLE:** If the cakes are domed on top, once they're completely cool, using a serrated knife and starting about 1 inch / 2.5cm in from the edge, carefully trim the tops to make them flat.

10. Place a cake layer, flat-side down, on a cake plate or stand.

11. Put about 2 cups / 460g of the buttercream into a piping bag fitted with a plain round tip with a ½-inch / 13mm or similar diameter. If the buttercream is too stiff to pipe, let it stand at room temperature for a few minutes to soften.

12. Holding the pastry tip about 1 inch / 2.5cm above the cake and starting about ¼ inch / 6mm from the edge, pipe a rounded ring of buttercream around the perimeter. Pipe zigzags of buttercream in the middle of the cake so it's completely covered. Using a small offset spatula, gently spread the zigzags of buttercream to fill in any gaps and connect them to the outer ring of buttercream, while leaving it intact.

13. Carefully place the second cake layer, flat-side up, on top, then gently wiggle it into the buttercream. Add more buttercream to the piping bag as needed. Repeat the above process but pipe the ring on the very edge of the cake. Once covered, use the tip of a small offset spatula to create some swooshes and texture on top of the cake (see How to Assemble, Frost, and Cut a Layer Cake, page 53).

14. Arrange a few large flowers and greenery on top of the cake, then fill in any remaining gaps with small flowers (see Tips for Working with Flowers, page 85). Add dehydrated fruit slices and sprinkle the crushed pistachios and freeze-dried raspberries on the buttercream, if desired. The cake (without foliage) keeps covered in the refrigerator for up to 5 days. Remove the cake about 1 hour before serving, so the buttercream has time to soften.

How to

ASSEMBLE, FROST, AND CUT A LAYER CAKE

As a self-taught baker, I learned how to assemble and frost cakes through a combination of watching online videos and, truthfully, a lot of trial and error. Over time, I finally figured it out—and now I feel like I actually know what I'm doing. I like to think of frosting cakes in three styles: fully exposed, naked, and fully covered. My signature style would have to be the fully exposed look—it's where you're not trying to hide your cake but instead are proud of it, just as much as your buttercream and filling. I'll be honest, I'm not one for perfectly polished cakes, and I don't aim for that. Even when I'm trying to create a more refined look with some piping, the cake still ends up imperfect and a bit whimsical. So don't overthink it!

HOW TO ASSEMBLE A LAYER CAKE

1. Some cakes are naturally more prone to doming, and in those cases, use a serrated knife to carefully trim off the dome, starting about 1 inch / 2.5cm in from the edge of the cake.

2. Place your first cake layer, flat-side down, on a cardboard round or a cake plate, and ideally on a turntable, as it makes frosting the cake easier.

3. Put some buttercream into a piping bag fitted with a plain round tip with a ½-inch / 13mm or similar diameter. When piping, hold the pastry tip about 1 inch / 2.5cm above the cake. This allows the buttercream to fall gently onto the cake with a thick, rounded shape, so it looks light, airy, and cloud-like. Starting about ¼ inch / 6mm from the edge, pipe a thick rounded line of buttercream around the perimeter of the bottom cake layer. If your cake includes a filling like jam or curd, pipe a second line of buttercream inside the first to prevent the filling from leaking out. I also pipe 2 concentric lines of buttercream if I'm making a fully exposed cake, because I want there to be fluffy rounded buttercream between the layers, but for naked and fully covered cakes, as well as mini cakes, one line of buttercream is usually enough.

4. Spoon the filling (if any) into the center of the cake and use a small offset spatula to spread it evenly so it reaches the buttercream perimeter and fully covers the middle of the cake.

5. Pipe zigzags of buttercream on top of the filling (or directly on the cake if there's no filling) so that it's completely covered, then use a small offset spatula to gently spread the buttercream zigzags to fill in any gaps and connect them to the buttercream perimeter. If making a fully exposed cake, be sure to keep the buttercream perimeter intact, so it maintains its round and fluffy appearance.

6. Carefully place the second cake layer, flat-side up, on top of the buttercream, then gently wiggle it into the buttercream.

THREE WAYS TO FROST A LAYER CAKE

Below you'll find three ways to frost a cake—fully exposed, which is my favorite, as well as naked and fully covered. Keep in mind that the technique used for a naked cake is essentially step one for a fully covered cake. For a naked cake, you cover the cake in a thin, even layer of buttercream, while for a fully covered cake, you apply the thin, even layer of buttercream, and then chill the cake before covering it in a thicker layer of buttercream. That thin, even layer of buttercream is called a crumb coat.

FULLY EXPOSED CAKE

Add more buttercream to the piping bag as needed. Holding the pastry tip about 1 inch / 2.5cm above the cake, pipe a ring of buttercream around the perimeter of the cake, then pipe zigzags of buttercream to fill the middle. Use a small offset spatula to gently spread the buttercream zigzags to fill in any gaps and connect them to the buttercream perimeter. Make sure the top of the cake is covered in a thick, even layer of buttercream and the outside edges are still round and fluffy. Use the tip of a small offset spatula to create some swooshes and texture on the top of the cake.

NAKED CAKE

Place a medium dollop of buttercream on the top of the cake, then use a small offset spatula to spread the buttercream evenly across the top and down the sides of the cake, covering the sponge completely. Take a straight-sided metal spatula or bench scraper and gently press the edge against the side of the cake. While spinning the turntable, apply light pressure to the spatula or bench scraper to gently scrape off any excess buttercream. This creates a thin, even layer that reveals some of the sponge beneath for that naked cake look.

FULLY COVERED CAKE

If making a fully covered cake, follow the instructions for the naked cake, so your cake is covered in a very thin layer of buttercream (the crumb coat), then refrigerate it, uncovered, for at least 15 minutes. Place a generous dollop of buttercream on top of the chilled cake, then use a small offset spatula to spread the buttercream evenly across the top, pushing any excess toward the edges. Add extra buttercream to the sides of the cake as needed and spread it so the cake is completely covered in an even layer of buttercream. For a decorative finish, use the tip of the spatula to create swooping motions on the surface of the cake—think of forming an inverted "C" or moon shape to mimic a meringue-like texture. For a playful touch, use a piping bag fitted with a very small star-shaped tip (about ¼ inch / 6mm in diameter) to pipe uneven swirls of buttercream around the edges of the cake. Aim for an imperfect look to keep it natural. If you don't have the right pastry tip, use small scissors to cut "teeth" into the bottom of the piping bag—it will create the same frilly accents.

CAKE CUTTING TIPS

When you're ready to serve your cake, you might find yourself in the very position I used to dread—having to cut it. Here are a few tips to keep your cake looking gorgeous.

Fill a glass with boiling water and fully submerge your knife blade in the water for a moment, then wipe it clean with a dry cloth. Immediately insert the tip of the knife where you want your slice, then gently cut all the way down, applying minimal pressure.

If your cake has jam in the center, avoid pulling the knife back up after slicing, as the jam will smear across the buttercream, and you won't have that perfect-looking cut. Instead, pull the knife outward in a smooth horizontal motion. For cakes with whipped cream frosting, insert the tip of the knife where you want to make your cut, then gently tippy-toe the knife, slicing outward. Avoid pressing down all at once, which can deflate the whipped cream or push it out between the cake layers.

Lastly, slice around any flowers, so they stay in place. If that's not possible, carefully remove the flowers before cutting, then place them back onto each slice.

EARL GREY BUTTERFLY PEA GINGER MINI CAKES

MAKES EIGHT 3-INCH / 7.5CM MINI CAKES

I'm obsessed with Earl Grey tea. I've always been a huge tea drinker—no coffee for me—and Earl Grey has long been my go-to. This light and airy sponge allows its unique flavor to truly shine with both Earl Grey–infused milk and an Earl Grey syrup to fully capture its essence. The buttercream is a twist on the classic American version, but it uses far less powdered sugar for a frosting that's smooth, creamy, and much less sweet. A double hit of ginger—I use both ground and crystallized—brings a cozy warmth to the buttercream, while butterfly pea flower powder contributes its vibrant blue hue, and is proof that you don't need artificial food coloring to create something eye-catching.

EARL GREY MILK

¾ cup plus 2 tablespoons / 210ml whole milk

¼ cup / 15g loose Earl Grey tea leaves

EARL GREY SYRUP

¾ cup / 180ml boiling water

5 tablespoons / 20g loose Earl Grey tea leaves

¾ cup / 150g granulated sugar

EARL GREY MINI CAKES

Canola oil spray or canola oil, for the pans

1¾ cups / 245g all-purpose flour

2 teaspoons baking powder

¼ teaspoon fine sea salt

⅓ cup / 80g sour cream, at room temperature

¾ teaspoon vanilla extract

1 stick plus 3 tablespoons / 143g unsalted butter, at room temperature and cut into small pieces

1 cup plus 2 tablespoons / 225g granulated sugar

3 large eggs, at room temperature

GINGER BUTTERFLY PEA BUTTERCREAM

2 cups / 240g powdered sugar, sifted

2 sticks / 226g unsalted butter, at room temperature and cut into small pieces

⅓ cup / 80ml heavy cream

5 teaspoons ground ginger

1 tablespoon finely chopped crystallized ginger

2 teaspoons butterfly pea flower powder

¼ teaspoon fine sea salt

ASSEMBLY

8 nasturtium flowers, for decorating

1. FOR THE EARL GREY MILK: In a small saucepan, warm the milk over low heat just until steam starts to rise from the surface; do not let it come to a simmer or boil. Remove from the heat, then stir in the Earl Grey tea leaves. Cover and let stand for 30 minutes.

2. Pour through a fine-mesh sieve set over a small bowl, pressing on the tea to extract as much flavor as possible (discard the tea leaves). Let the milk cool completely.

3. FOR THE EARL GREY SYRUP: In a small bowl, combine the boiling water and Earl Grey tea leaves and let stand for 5 minutes.

4. Pour through a fine-mesh sieve set over a small saucepan, pressing on the tea to extract as much flavor as possible (discard the tea leaves). Add the granulated sugar, set the pan over medium-high heat, and bring to a simmer. Continue simmering until reduced to a thick syrup, about 4 minutes. Remove from the heat and let the syrup cool to room temperature.

5. FOR THE EARL GREY MINI CAKES: Set a rack in the middle of the oven and preheat to 325°F / 160°C. Spray or brush the sides of eight 3-inch / 7.5cm round mini cake pans with canola oil, then line the bottoms with parchment paper.

6. Sift the flour and baking powder into a small bowl. Add the salt.

7. In a small bowl, combine ½ cup plus 2 tablespoons / 150ml of the Earl Grey milk, the sour cream, and vanilla and whisk to combine.

RECIPE CONTINUES

8. In a stand mixer fitted with the paddle, beat the butter on medium speed, scraping down the bottom and sides of the bowl as needed, until creamy, about 2 minutes. Add the granulated sugar and 2 tablespoons plus 1 teaspoon of the Earl Grey syrup and beat on medium-high speed, scraping the bowl as needed, until pale and fluffy, about 3 minutes. Scrape the bowl, then add the eggs, one at a time, and beat on medium speed, scraping the bowl before each addition and again at the end, until fully incorporated. Scrape the bowl. On low speed, add the flour mixture in three batches, alternating with the Earl Grey milk mixture in two batches and scraping before each addition. Mix just until there are no streaks. Do not overmix!

9. Divide the batter evenly among the prepared pans. Tap the pans on the counter to even out the batter, then arrange the filled cake pans on a baking sheet. Bake until the tops spring back when lightly pressed and a skewer inserted in the center of the cakes comes out clean, 17 to 20 minutes.

10. Let the cakes cool in the pans on a wire rack for 30 minutes. Jiggle the pans upside down to release the cakes. Remove the parchment paper. Flip the cakes so they are right-side up on the rack. Let cool completely.

11. FOR THE GINGER BUTTERFLY PEA BUTTERCREAM: In a stand mixer fitted with the paddle, mix the powdered sugar, butter, heavy cream, ground ginger, crystallized ginger, butterfly pea flower powder, and salt on low speed just until combined, about 30 seconds. Beat on high speed, scraping the bowl as needed, until light, fluffy, and slightly shiny, about 10 minutes. Mix on low speed for 1 to 2 minutes more to remove any air bubbles and make the buttercream easier to pipe.

12. TO ASSEMBLE: If any of the mini cakes have domed tops, once they are completely cool, use a serrated knife to slice off the domes, so the cakes are flat and even. Place one mini cake, flat-side down, on a plate or preferably on a turntable for easier piping.

13. Fill a piping bag fitted with a small to medium-size V-shaped Saint Honoré tip with the buttercream. Hold the pastry tip at a slight angle and with the V-shaped opening facing up, then start in the center of the mini cake and gently squeeze the piping bag while moving it outward, before coming back to the center to create a curved petal. Continue piping, while rotating the cake and slightly overlapping the petals, to create a flower shape. Repeat to frost the remaining mini cakes. Arrange a nasturtium flower, upside down, on each cake. The mini cakes (without flowers) keep covered in the refrigerator for up to 2 days. Remove the cakes about 2 hours before serving, so the buttercream has time to soften.

CHAMOMILE CAKE

MAKES ONE 10-INCH / 25CM TWO-LAYER CAKE

I've always used chamomile flowers as decoration on my cakes. I love that they're so playful and bright, but as I started drinking more chamomile tea, I got curious about integrating its flavor into the actual cakes. The chamomile infusion in this recipe is subtle, but since the tea is in both the sponge and the whipped cream, its citrusy, fruity notes really shine. I like to add a layer of my strawberry sumac jam, which has the warmth and sweetness of a classic strawberry jam but extra tartness thanks to sumac. If you're short on time or don't want to make homemade jam, add 2¼ teaspoons sumac to 1½ cups / 450g store-bought strawberry jam.

CHAMOMILE CAKE

Canola oil spray or canola oil, for the pans
1½ cups plus 1 tablespoon / 375ml whole milk, plus more as needed
6 tablespoons / 10g loose chamomile tea leaves
3 cups / 420g all-purpose flour
4 teaspoons baking powder
¼ teaspoon fine sea salt
6 large eggs, at room temperature
2 cups plus 2 tablespoons / 425g granulated sugar
1½ sticks / 168g unsalted butter
2 tablespoons canola oil

CHAMOMILE WHIPPED CREAM

2¼ cups / 540ml heavy cream
6 tablespoons / 10g loose chamomile tea leaves
¼ cup / 30g powdered sugar, sifted

ASSEMBLY

1½ cups / 405g Strawberry Sumac Jam (recipe follows)
Strawberries (optional), hulled and quartered, for decorating
Powdered sugar, for sifting

1. FOR THE CHAMOMILE CAKE: Set a rack in the middle of the oven and preheat to 350°F / 180°C. Spray or brush the sides of two 10-inch / 25cm round cake pans with canola oil, then line the bottoms with parchment paper.

2. In a small saucepan, warm the milk over medium heat just until steam starts to rise from the surface; do not let it come to a simmer or bubble. Remove from the heat, then stir in the chamomile tea leaves, cover, and let stand for at least 30 minutes at room temperature but preferably overnight in the refrigerator.

3. Pour through a fine-mesh sieve set over a small bowl, pressing on the tea to extract as much flavor as possible (discard the tea leaves). Measure the milk, and if it's not 1½ cups plus 1 tablespoon / 375ml, add more plain milk as needed.

4. Sift the flour and baking powder into a medium bowl. Add the salt.

5. In a stand mixer fitted with the whisk, whip the eggs on high speed for 30 seconds. On medium speed, gradually add the granulated sugar. Once all the sugar is added, whip on high speed until pale, fluffy, and almost tripled in volume, about 7 minutes.

6. Meanwhile, in a small saucepan, combine the chamomile-infused milk and the butter and heat over medium-low heat, stirring occasionally, until the butter is melted. Add the canola oil and stir to incorporate. Remove from the heat.

7. Once the eggs are whipped, scrape down the bottom and sides of the bowl. Add the flour mixture in three batches, and mix on low speed, scraping the bowl before each addition, just until there are no streaks. Do not overmix!

8. Add about one-fifth of the egg and flour mixture to the warm milk mixture and gently fold. Add this to the remaining egg and flour mixture in the stand mixer, then mix on low speed until just combined, about 20 seconds.

RECIPE CONTINUES

Scrape the bowl, then mix for about 10 seconds to make sure it's fully combined.

9. Divide the batter evenly between the prepared pans, smoothing the tops. Bake for 15 minutes, then quickly rotate the pans and continue baking until the cakes are golden on top and a skewer inserted in the center of each cake comes out clean, about 15 minutes more.

10. Let the cakes cool in the pans on a wire rack for 20 minutes. Carefully run a small offset spatula between the edges of the pans and the cakes, then flip the pans onto the rack and tap them to make sure the cakes are released. Remove the parchment paper. Leave the cakes upside down and let cool completely.

11. FOR THE CHAMOMILE WHIPPED CREAM: In a small saucepan, warm the heavy cream over medium heat just until steam starts to rise from the surface; do not let it come to a simmer or bubble. Remove from the heat, then stir in the chamomile tea leaves, cover, and let stand for 30 minutes.

12. Pour through a fine-mesh sieve set over a small bowl, pressing on the tea to extract as much flavor as possible (discard the tea leaves). Cover and refrigerate until cold, at least 1 hour.

13. Once cold, transfer the tea-infused cream to a stand mixer fitted with the whisk. Add the powdered sugar and whip on medium-high speed for 3 minutes, then increase the speed to high and whip until very stiff peaks form, 2 to 3 minutes more.

14. TO ASSEMBLE: If the cakes are domed on top, once they're completely cool, using a serrated knife and starting about 1 inch / 2.5cm in from the edge, carefully trim the tops to make them flat.

15. Place a cake layer, flat-side down, on a cake plate or stand.

16. Using a rubber spatula, put a large dollop of the chamomile whipped cream on top of the cake. Use a small offset spatula to spread the whipped cream on top of the cake, then use the tip of the spatula to create some swooshes and texture on top of the cake.

17. Add the strawberry sumac jam on top of the whipped cream and spread it almost to the edge so some jam drips down the sides, creating a generous, homemade look. Arrange the quartered strawberries, if using, on top. Gently place the other cake layer, flat-side up, on top, trying not to press down, so the whipped cream doesn't come out the sides too much. Sift some powdered sugar on top before serving. The cake is best the day it's assembled, but it keeps covered in the refrigerator for up to 1 day.

Strawberry Sumac Jam

MAKES 4 CUPS / 1.1KG

3 pounds / 1.4kg hulled strawberries, fresh or thawed frozen (about 12 cups), quartered
4 cups / 800g sugar
2 tablespoons sumac
Juice of 2 lemons

1. In a large bowl, combine the strawberries and sugar and toss to coat the fruit. Cover and refrigerate for at least 30 minutes but preferably overnight.

2. Put two small plates in the freezer.

3. Transfer the macerated strawberries to a large Dutch oven or heavy-bottomed saucepan, set over medium-high heat, and cook, stirring frequently to keep the fruit from burning. As the mixture comes to a boil, use a large stainless steel spoon to skim off the light pink foam that rises to the top.

4. When the jam starts to feel a bit thick, scoop a spoonful onto one of the frozen plates and wait 1 to 2 minutes for it to come to room temperature. Tip the plate from side to side. If the jam is ready, it will hold its shape on the plate rather than run down it. If you're not sure, try running a spoon through the jam on the plate—if it holds the line, it's ready. Technically, jam should register about 220°F / 104°C, and if you're new to jam making, using a thermometer can be really helpful, but part of the fun is relying on your senses. The jam should have a smooth texture studded with strawberry seeds and some chunks of fruit. If needed, continue cooking the jam until it sets on the second frozen plate.

5. Once the jam passes the plate test, add the sumac and lemon juice, then remove it from the heat. If you want to seal the jam in jars for longer term storage, do so while it's still hot (see How to Can Jams and Curds, page 187).

6. Otherwise, let the jam stand in the pot, without stirring, to cool and thicken for about 30 minutes, then transfer it to jars or airtight containers but do not cover. Let the jam cool to room temperature, then cover and refrigerate for up to 2 weeks. You can cool the jam in the refrigerator, but it's important to allow the jam to fully cool before covering, as condensation could drip back into your beautiful work and loosen the texture.

RASPBERRY VANILLA SPONGE ROLL

MAKES ONE 13-INCH / 33CM SPONGE ROLL CAKE

If I picture myself eating cake while sitting by a fireplace on a cold and rainy day with a good book and a cup of tea, I'm definitely eating this sponge roll. There is nothing more comforting than a light and fluffy sponge, overflowing raspberry jam, and too much vanilla bean whipped cream. To achieve the cake's perfect spongy texture, be careful to not overmix the batter once the flour is added. When making the whipped cream, don't substitute vanilla extract for the vanilla bean paste—you won't get the same warm vanilla notes that this cake needs!

Canola oil spray or canola oil, for the pans
Powdered sugar, for dusting
1 cup / 140g all-purpose flour
2 teaspoons baking powder
6 large eggs, at room temperature
¼ teaspoon fine sea salt
1½ cups / 300g granulated sugar
4 tablespoons / 55g unsalted butter
4 cups / 400g Vanilla Bean Whipped Cream (page 221)
About 1 cup / 300g raspberry jam, homemade (page 95) or store-bought

1. Set a rack in the middle of the oven and preheat to 400°F / 200°C. Spray or brush the bottom and sides of one 13 × 18-inch / 33 × 45cm baking sheet with canola oil and line the bottom with parchment paper. Dust a similarly sized clean tea towel with powdered sugar and set it near the oven.

2. Sift the flour and baking powder into a small bowl.

3. In a stand mixer fitted with the paddle, beat the eggs and salt on high speed until fully combined, about 1 minute. Scrape down the bottom and sides of the bowl, then add the granulated sugar and beat until thick, pale yellow, and doubled in volume, about 5 minutes.

4. Remove the bowl from the stand mixer and scrape it again. Add the flour mixture in three batches and gently fold with a rubber spatula just until there are no streaks. Do not overmix!

5. In a small saucepan, bring the butter to a boil over medium-low heat. Carefully pour the hot butter into the batter and use the spatula to gently fold just until incorporated.

6. Gently spread the batter evenly in the prepared pan, smoothing the top. Bake until the cake is golden brown on top and feels spongy when lightly pressed, about 10 minutes.

7. Carefully flip the cake onto the powdered sugar–dusted tea towel. Remove the parchment paper.

8. Starting on one of the short sides, quickly but gently roll the cake into a tight spiral. Arrange the roll so the seam is on the bottom and let cool for about 30 minutes while you prepare the whipped cream as directed in that recipe.

9. Gently unroll the cake. It will have deflated a bit. Spread a generous layer of jam evenly across the entire surface of the cake. Carefully spread a generous layer of whipped cream across the entire surface of the cake, completely covering the jam but keeping the layers separate. Carefully roll the cake back into a spiral, making sure the seam is on the bottom.

10. Dust with powdered sugar and serve right away. The cake is best the day it's assembled, but it keeps covered in the refrigerator for up to 1 day.

LA BONNE CUISINE D'AUJOURD'HUI

SALTED DARK CHOCOLATE ESPRESSO SHEET CAKE

MAKES ONE 9 × 13-INCH / 23 × 33CM TWO-LAYER SHEET CAKE

I call this cake the adult version of a childhood birthday cake. Using dark chocolate and espresso brings in more depth, while adding chocolate chips to the buttercream adds an element of surprise that truly makes the cake. It's become a classic at the bakery. The buttercream needs to be stiff enough to hold its shape when stacking the second cake layer on top, so you'll need your muscles when it comes time for piping. Be sure to use a pastry tip with an opening large enough to let the chocolate chips through. If you're a coffee lover, I recommend sticking to instant espresso in your buttercream, but if you don't want to fuss with both coffee and espresso, just instant coffee will do.

CHOCOLATE CAKE

- Canola oil spray or canola oil, for the pans
- 1½ teaspoons instant coffee
- 1½ cups / 360ml boiling water
- 2¾ cups / 385g all-purpose flour
- ⅔ cup / 55g unsweetened Dutch-process cocoa powder
- 1 tablespoon baking soda
- 1¾ teaspoons baking powder
- 1 teaspoon fine sea salt
- 1 cup / 240ml buttermilk, at room temperature
- ½ cup / 120g sour cream, at room temperature
- 2½ cups / 500g granulated sugar
- ¾ cup plus 2 tablespoons / 210ml canola oil
- 3 large eggs, at room temperature
- 1 tablespoon vanilla extract

SALTED DARK CHOCOLATE ESPRESSO BUTTERCREAM

- 2 teaspoons instant espresso
- 2 tablespoons boiling water
- 2 pounds / 910g dark chocolate, preferably 72% cacao, chopped
- 8½ cups / 1,020g powdered sugar
- 1⅓ cups / 105g unsweetened Dutch-process cocoa powder
- 4 sticks / 452g unsalted butter, at room temperature and cut into small pieces
- 3 cups / 720g sour cream, at room temperature
- 1 teaspoon fine sea salt
- 1 teaspoon Maldon sea salt
- ⅓ cup / 60g mini chocolate chips

ASSEMBLY

- Meringue Letters (optional; recipe follows), for decorating

1. FOR THE CHOCOLATE CAKE: Set a rack in the middle of the oven and preheat to 350°F / 180°C. Spray or brush the bottom and sides of two 9 × 13-inch / 23 × 33cm baking sheets with canola oil and line the bottoms with parchment paper.

2. In a small bowl, combine the instant coffee and boiling water and stir to dissolve. Place in the refrigerator to cool.

3. Sift the flour, cocoa powder, baking soda, and baking powder into a medium bowl. Add the salt.

4. In another small bowl, combine the buttermilk and sour cream and whisk to fully combine.

5. In a stand mixer fitted with the paddle, beat the granulated sugar and canola oil on medium speed until they're combined and the mixture looks like wet sand, about 30 seconds. Scrape down the bottom and sides of the bowl, then add the eggs, one at a time, and beat, scraping the bowl before each addition and again at the end, until fully incorporated. Add the vanilla and beat until incorporated, about 30 seconds. Scrape the bowl. On low speed, add the flour mixture in four batches, alternating with the buttermilk mixture in three batches, and scraping the bowl before each addition. Mix just until there are no streaks. Do not overmix! Gradually add the cooled instant coffee, then mix for 30 seconds more. Scrape the bowl one final time. The batter will be very dark in color and quite thin.

6. Carefully divide the batter evenly between the prepared pans. Bake for about 15 minutes, then quickly rotate the pans and bake until the cakes spring back

when lightly pressed and a skewer inserted in the center of each cake comes out clean, 15 to 20 minutes more. The cakes should be soft and fluffy.

7. Let the cakes cool in the pans on wire racks for 30 minutes. Carefully run a small offset spatula between the edges of the pans and the cakes, then flip the pans onto the racks and tap them to make sure the cakes are released. Remove the parchment paper. Use a second rack or a large platter to flip the cakes so they are right-side up on the rack. Let cool completely.

8. **FOR THE SALTED DARK CHOCOLATE ESPRESSO BUTTERCREAM:** In a small bowl, combine the instant espresso and boiling water and stir to dissolve. Place in the refrigerator to cool.

9. Fill a medium saucepan with about 1 inch / 2.5cm of water and bring to a simmer over medium-low heat. Add the dark chocolate to a large heatproof bowl, then set the bowl over the pan of simmering water, making sure the water does not touch the bottom of the bowl. Warm the chocolate, stirring occasionally, until melted. Remove the bowl from the pan (careful—it will be warm!) and use a clean kitchen towel to carefully wipe any condensation from the bottom of the bowl. Set aside to cool.

10. Sift the powdered sugar and cocoa powder into a large bowl.

11. In a stand mixer fitted with the paddle, beat the butter on medium-high speed until pale and fluffy, about 3 minutes. Add the powdered sugar mixture in four batches and mix on low speed, scraping the bowl before each addition, until completely incorporated. The consistency will be like Play-Doh. Beat on medium speed until smooth, about 30 seconds more.

12. Add the sour cream to the cooled chocolate and stir to completely combine. Add to the butter mixture and beat on medium speed for 30 seconds, then increase the speed to high and beat until pale in color, light, and fluffy, about 2 minutes. Scrape the bowl, then add the cooled espresso and the fine salt and beat until smoother and lighter in color, about 3 minutes. Add the Maldon salt and beat on medium-high speed just until fully incorporated, about 15 seconds. Scoop three-quarters of the frosting—about 9 cups / 2.250g—into a large bowl and set it aside. Add the mini chocolate chips to the stand mixer and beat briefly just to incorporate the chips into the remaining 3 cups / 750g of buttercream. The frosting will be slightly soft, so cover both portions and refrigerate for 30 minutes to firm up. When ready to assemble the cake, let the buttercream sit at room temperature until spreadable, about 15 minutes. (The chocolate chip buttercream will be used between the cake layers, while the buttercream without chips will be used to cover and decorate the cake.)

13. **TO ASSEMBLE:** Place a cake layer on a large platter or board.

14. Put 2 to 3 cups / 500 to 750g of the chocolate chip buttercream into a piping bag fitted with a plain round tip with a ½-inch / 13mm or similar diameter.

RECIPE CONTINUES

15. Holding the pastry tip about 1 inch / 2.5cm above the cake and starting about ¼ inch / 6mm from the edge, pipe a rounded line of buttercream around the perimeter. Pipe zigzags of buttercream in the middle of the cake so it's completely covered. Using a small offset spatula, gently spread the buttercream zigzags to fill in any gaps and connect them to the buttercream perimeter, while leaving it intact.

16. Carefully place the second cake layer, flat-side up, on top, then gently wiggle it into the buttercream. Empty the piping bag, then fill it with the chip-free buttercream. Pipe zigzags of buttercream to completely cover the top of the cake. Using a small offset spatula, spread the buttercream evenly across the top and down the sides of the cake, so it's completely covered. Using a large metal spatula or a bench scraper, gently press against the sides of the cake to smooth the buttercream into a thin, even layer to completely cover the outside of the cake. This is your crumb coat. You should be able to see some of the cake underneath. Put the cake in the refrigerator for 15 minutes to firm up.

17. Using a rubber spatula, put a large dollop of the chip-free buttercream on top of the cake. Use the small offset spatula to spread it evenly, pushing any excess toward the edges of the cake. Add more buttercream to the edges of the cake as needed and use the small offset spatula to smooth the buttercream into an even layer on the top and sides of the cake. Transfer the remaining chip-free buttercream to a piping bag fitted with a small star tip, then pipe uneven swirls of buttercream along the top and bottom edges of the cake. If desired, pipe additional crisscross decorations on the sides of the cake (see How to Assemble, Frost, and Cut a Layer Cake, page 53).

18. Arrange the meringue letters on top of the cake, if desired. The cake keeps covered in the refrigerator for up to 5 days. Remove the cake about 2 hours before serving, so the buttercream has time to soften.

Meringue Letters

MAKES ENOUGH MERINGUE LETTERS (OR NUMBERS)
TO DECORATE SEVERAL CAKES, WITH EXTRA FOR SNACKING

Distilled white vinegar
105g egg whites (about 3 large), at room temperature
¼ teaspoon cream of tartar
Pinch of fine sea salt
¾ cup / 150g sugar
½ teaspoon vanilla extract

1. Set a rack in the middle of the oven and preheat to 200°F / 90°C. Line two 13 × 18-inch / 33 × 45cm baking sheets with parchment paper.

2. Use a paper towel and about ¼ teaspoon of white vinegar to wipe all over the surface of the bowl of a stand mixer, making sure there aren't any traces of liquid or fat.

3. In the clean bowl of the stand mixer fitted with the whisk, whip the egg whites, cream of tartar, and salt on low speed until the egg whites are frothy, 1 to 2 minutes. On high speed, gradually add the sugar, 1 tablespoon at a time, and whip, making sure the sugar fully dissolves into the egg white mixture before adding more, about 20 seconds per addition. Once all the sugar has been added, whip until the meringue is thick, glossy, and tripled in volume, 5 to 7 minutes. Scrape down the bottom and sides of the bowl, then add the vanilla and whip on low speed for about 30 seconds to incorporate.

4. Fill a piping bag fitted with a plain round tip with a ½-inch / 13mm or similar diameter with the meringue. Keeping the size of your cake and how you want the decorations to appear in mind, pipe the desired letters, numbers, or other designs directly on the prepared baking sheet. Leave about 1 inch / 2.5cm of space between them. Once you have your desired decorations, pipe any remaining meringue into rosettes or other shapes.

5. Bake for 1 hour, then turn off the oven without opening the door. Leave the meringue letters in the oven and let them dry out while the oven cools completely, which allows them to set without cracking.

6. Use the meringue letters to decorate cakes and other desserts. The meringue letters keep in an airtight container at cool room temperature for up to 1 week.

CARDAMOM POLENTA ROSE WATER BUNDT CAKE

MAKES ONE 12-CUP / 2.8L BUNDT CAKE

I created this recipe specifically for a Bundt pan—not just for its aesthetics, but because it perfectly suits the cake's texture. Unlike light and airy sponge cakes, this cake is hearty, rich, and dense. Warm, comforting cardamom pairs beautifully with golden polenta, giving the crumb a pleasing crunch. The rose water glaze adds a subtle floral sweetness that enhances the spice, while a sprinkle of dried roses ties it all together with a touch of elegance and aroma.

CARDAMOM POLENTA BUNDT CAKE

Softened unsalted butter and flour, for the pan
5 tablespoons / 75g unsalted butter, at room temperature and cut into small pieces
1¾ cups / 245g all-purpose flour
1½ cups / 200g stone-ground medium-grind cornmeal
¾ cup / 150g granulated sugar
¾ cup / 150g (packed) light brown sugar
1 tablespoon ground cardamom
1 teaspoon baking soda
1 teaspoon fine sea salt
2 large eggs, at room temperature
2 large egg yolks, at room temperature
2¼ cups / 540ml buttermilk, at room temperature
1 cup / 240ml canola oil

ROSE WATER GLAZE

1½ cups plus 3 tablespoons / 200g powdered sugar
1 tablespoon rose water
2 tablespoons whole milk
⅛ teaspoon grated lemon zest (from 1 medium lemon)
⅛ teaspoon fine sea salt
1 teaspoon dried organic rosebuds and rose petals, for serving

1. FOR THE CARDAMOM POLENTA BUNDT CAKE: Set a rack in the middle of the oven and preheat to 350°F / 180°C. Generously butter a 12-cup / 2.8L Bundt pan, then dust it with a thick layer of flour.

2. In a stand mixer fitted with the paddle, beat the butter, flour, cornmeal, granulated sugar, brown sugar, cardamom, baking soda, and salt on medium-low speed until fully combined, about 2 minutes. Scrape down the bottom and sides of the bowl. Gradually add the whole eggs and egg yolks and beat, scraping the bowl as needed, until fully incorporated. Scrape the bowl, then beat for 15 seconds more. Gradually add the buttermilk, followed by the canola oil, and beat until fully incorporated.

3. Pour the batter into the prepared pan, smoothing the top. Bake until the top is lightly golden and a skewer inserted near the center of the cake comes out clean, 45 to 50 minutes. Be careful not to overbake this cake or it will dry out!

4. Let the cake cool in the pan on a wire rack for 30 minutes. Carefully flip the pan onto the rack and tap it to make sure the cake is released. Remove the pan and let the cake cool completely.

5. FOR THE ROSE WATER GLAZE: Sift the powdered sugar into the bowl of a stand mixer, then add the rose water and use the whisk attachment to mix on low speed for 15 seconds. Scrape the bowl, then add the milk, lemon zest, and salt and whip on medium-high speed for 30 seconds. If the glaze seems too runny, let it stand for a few minutes to firm up.

6. Place the cake on a wire rack set inside a baking sheet.

7. Transfer the glaze to a small, spouted measuring cup, then slowly pour it over the top of the Bundt, using a small spoon to scoop the glaze onto the cake as needed so it drizzles down the sides.

8. Before the glaze sets, sprinkle the cake with dried rosebuds and rose petals and let set for a few minutes before serving. The cake keeps covered in the refrigerator for up to 1 day.

COCONUT WHITE CHOCOLATE CAKE

MAKES ONE 8-INCH / 23CM TWO-LAYER CAKE

This cake is one of my favorites to make around the holidays, as it reminds me of a snowy and cold day. It's also soft, moist, spongy, and super easy to make! The cream cheese buttercream provides a tangy contrast to the sweetness of the white chocolate and coconut, while its soft, velvety texture helps the coconut flakes stick beautifully. If it's warm outside and your buttercream is a bit too soft to spread on the cake, 15 to 20 minutes in the fridge will firm it up.

COCONUT CAKE

Canola oil spray or canola oil, for the pans
2½ cups / 350g all-purpose flour
2 teaspoons baking powder
½ teaspoon fine sea salt
1 stick / 113g unsalted butter, at room temperature and cut into small pieces
1 cup / 200g granulated sugar
4 large eggs, at room temperature
1 teaspoon vanilla extract
1¼ cups / 300ml canned coconut milk
2 cups / 170g sweetened shredded coconut

WHITE CHOCOLATE CREAM CHEESE BUTTERCREAM

Distilled white vinegar
6¼ ounces / 175g white chocolate, chopped
1 stick / 113g unsalted butter, at room temperature and cut into small pieces
2¼ cups / 270g powdered sugar, sifted
2 cups / 450g cream cheese or fromage frais, at room temperature and cut into small pieces
Pinch of fine sea salt

ASSEMBLY

2 cups / 170g sweetened shredded coconut
1 small spray rosebud, preferably fuchsia, with stem for decorating

1. FOR THE COCONUT CAKE: Set a rack in the middle of the oven and preheat to 350°F / 180°C. Spray or brush the sides of two 8-inch / 23cm round cake pans with canola oil, then line the bottoms with parchment paper.

2. Sift the flour and baking powder into a medium bowl. Add the salt.

3. In a stand mixer fitted with the paddle, beat the butter and granulated sugar on medium-high speed until light and fluffy, about 3 minutes. Add the eggs, one at a time, and beat on medium speed, scraping down the bottom and sides of the bowl before each addition and again at the end, until fully incorporated. Add the vanilla and beat for 30 seconds to incorporate, then scrape the bowl. On low speed, add the flour mixture in three batches, alternating with the coconut milk in two batches and scraping the bowl before each addition. Mix just until there are no streaks. Do not overmix!

4. Remove the bowl from the mixer, then fold in the shredded coconut with a rubber spatula just until incorporated.

5. Divide the batter evenly between the prepared pans, smoothing the tops. Bake until a skewer inserted in the center of each cake comes out clean, about 30 minutes.

6. Let the cakes cool in the pans on a wire rack for 15 minutes. Flip the pans onto the racks and tap them to make sure the cakes are released. Remove the parchment paper. Leave the cakes upside down and let cool completely.

7. FOR THE WHITE CHOCOLATE CREAM CHEESE BUTTERCREAM: Use a paper towel and about ¼ teaspoon of white vinegar to wipe all over the surface of a large heatproof bowl, making sure there aren't any traces of liquid or fat.

8. Fill a medium saucepan with about 1 inch / 2.5cm of water and bring to a simmer over medium-low heat. Add the white chocolate to the clean heatproof bowl, then set the bowl over the pan of simmering water, making sure the water does not touch the bottom of the bowl. Warm the white chocolate, stirring occasionally, until melted. Remove the bowl from the pan (careful—it will

be warm!) and use a clean kitchen towel to carefully wipe any condensation from the bottom of the bowl. Let cool slightly, just until warm to the touch.

9. In a stand mixer fitted with the paddle, beat the butter on medium-high speed until light and fluffy, about 3 minutes. Gradually add the powdered sugar and mix on low speed, scraping the bowl as needed, until incorporated, then increase the speed to medium and beat until smooth, about 30 seconds. Starting on low speed, gradually add the cream cheese, a few small pieces at a time, then increase the speed to medium and continue beating until creamy, smooth, and lighter in color, about 2 minutes total. On medium-high speed, gradually drizzle in the melted white chocolate and continue beating until fully incorporated, about 2 minutes total. Scrape the bowl, then add the salt and beat on medium-high speed until the buttercream is light and fluffy, about 4 minutes.

10. TO ASSEMBLE: Once the cakes are completely cool, use a second rack or a plate to flip them, so they are right-side up on the rack. If the cakes are domed on top, using a serrated knife and starting about 1 inch / 2.5cm in from the edge, carefully trim the tops to make them flat.

11. Place a cake layer, flat-side down, on a cake plate or stand. Using a rubber spatula, put about 2 cups / 400g of the buttercream on top of the cake. Use a small offset spatula to spread the buttercream evenly over the entire top surface.

12. Carefully place the other cake layer, flat-side up, on top, then gently wiggle it into the buttercream. Using the rubber spatula, put the remaining buttercream on top of the cake. Use the small offset spatula to spread the buttercream on the top and sides of the cake, smoothing it to completely cover the cake. Gently press the shredded coconut onto the buttercream, covering the top and sides of the cake.

13. Gently press the stem of the spray rosebud in the center of the cake. The cake (without the spray rosebud) keeps covered in the refrigerator for up to 3 days. Remove the cake about 2 hours before serving, so the buttercream has time to soften.

VEGAN VANILLA EARL GREY BLACKBERRY MINI CAKES

MAKES EIGHT 3-INCH / 7.5CM MINI TWO-LAYER CAKES

If you need a classic vanilla sponge cake to bake for the rest of your life, make it this one—whether you are vegan or not. You may not even notice it's vegan, as it's incredibly soft and spongy and stays moist for several days. At the bakery, we use this vanilla bean–infused sponge with all kinds of frostings and jams. It truly goes with anything, but I find myself craving this particular combination of Earl Grey frosting and blackberry jam. I eat it often, and it's my go-to cake for any occasion.

VANILLA BEAN MINI CAKES

Canola oil spray or canola oil, for the pans
1 cup plus 1 tablespoon / 255ml soy milk, at room temperature
1½ teaspoons apple cider vinegar
2½ cups plus 2 tablespoons / 370g all-purpose flour
1¾ teaspoons baking powder
¾ teaspoon baking soda
¼ teaspoon fine sea salt
1¼ cups plus 2 tablespoons / 275g granulated sugar
¾ cup plus 2 tablespoons / 210ml canola oil
¾ cup / 195g unsweetened applesauce
1 teaspoon vanilla bean paste

EARL GREY FROSTING

¼ cup / 60ml soy milk, plus more as needed
1½ teaspoons loose Earl Grey tea leaves, plus 1 tablespoon loose Earl Grey tea leaves, finely ground
1 stick plus 5 tablespoons / 183g plant-based butter, cold and cut into small pieces
5¾ cups / 690g powdered sugar, sifted
¾ teaspoon grated lemon zest (from 1 medium lemon)
½ teaspoon fine sea salt

ASSEMBLY

½ to ¾ cup / 150 to 225g blackberry jam, homemade (page 185) or store-bought
Small flowers and greenery (see page 88), for decorating
Dehydrated fruit slices (page 103), crushed pistachios (page 83), and crushed freeze-dried raspberries (page 83), for decorating (optional)

1. FOR THE VANILLA BEAN MINI CAKES: Set a rack in the middle of the oven and preheat to 350°F / 180°C. Spray or brush the sides of eight 3-inch / 7.5cm round mini cake pans with canola oil, then line the bottoms with parchment paper.

2. Pour the soy milk and apple cider vinegar into a small bowl and let stand without mixing. This will slowly curdle into your vegan "buttermilk."

3. Sift the flour, baking powder, and baking soda into a medium bowl. Add the salt.

4. In a stand mixer fitted with the paddle, beat the granulated sugar, canola oil, applesauce, and vanilla bean paste on high speed until fully combined, about 2 minutes. Scrape down the bottom and sides of the bowl. On low speed, add the flour mixture in three batches, alternating with the "buttermilk" mixture in two batches and scraping the bowl before each addition. Mix just until there are no streaks. Do not overmix!

5. Divide the batter evenly among the prepared pans. Tap the pans on the counter to even out the batter, then arrange the filled cake pans on a baking sheet. Bake until a skewer inserted into the center of each cake comes out clean, about 30 minutes.

6. Let the cakes cool in the pans on a wire rack for 15 minutes. Jiggle the pans upside down to release the cakes. Remove the parchment paper. Flip the cakes so they are right-side up on the rack. Let cool completely.

7. FOR THE EARL GREY FROSTING: In a small saucepan, bring the soy milk to a simmer over low heat. Remove from the heat, then stir in the 1½ teaspoons of whole Earl Grey tea leaves, cover, and let stand for 30 minutes.

RECIPE CONTINUES

8. Pour through a fine-mesh sieve set over a small bowl, pressing on the tea to extract as much flavor as possible (discard the tea leaves). Cover and refrigerate until cold, about 1 hour.

9. In a stand mixer fitted with the paddle, beat the plant-based butter on medium-high speed, scraping down the bottom and sides of the bowl as needed, until creamy and lighter in color, about 3 minutes. Scrape the bowl, then add the powdered sugar in three batches and mix on low speed, scraping the bowl as needed, until fully combined. Add the cold Earl Grey tea–infused soy milk and beat on medium speed until light and fluffy, about 1 minute. Scrape the bowl, then add the ground Earl Grey tea, lemon zest, and salt and beat on medium-high speed until fluffy and easily spreadable, about 1 minute. If the frosting is too stiff, add more plain soy milk, 1 tablespoon at a time, until it's spreadable. If the frosting seems soft, wait—it will firm up after a few minutes.

10. TO ASSEMBLE: If any mini cakes have domed tops, once they are completely cool, use a serrated knife to slice off the domes, so the cakes are flat and even. Carefully cut each cake horizontally in half to create two layers. Place the cake bottoms, flat-sides down, on a cake board or serving plate.

11. Put about 1 cup / 200g of the frosting into a piping bag fitted with a plain round tip with a ½-inch / 13mm or similar diameter. Holding the pastry tip about 1 inch / 2.5cm above a cake bottom and starting from the edge, pipe a rounded ring of frosting around the perimeter. Spoon about 1 tablespoon of blackberry jam in the middle. Pipe a dollop of frosting on top of the jam, then use a small offset spatula to gently spread the dollop so it covers the top of the cake, while leaving the frosting ring intact. Repeat with the remaining cake bottoms.

12. Carefully place the cake tops, flat-sides up, on top of the cake bottoms, then gently wiggle them into the frosting. Add more frosting to the piping bag as needed. Repeat the above process to frost the tops of the mini cakes but skip the jam.

13. If desired, you can add a dollop of frosting and jam to the top of each mini cake: Holding the pastry tip about 1 inch / 2.5cm above a cake, pipe a dollop of frosting in the middle. Repeat for the remaining cakes. Dip a teaspoon in hot water, then use it to create divots or "bowls" in each dollop of frosting. Use two small spoons to plop some jam in each frosting "bowl."

14. Arrange a small flower and some greenery on each cake (see Tips for Working with Flowers, page 85). Add a slice of dehydrated fruit and sprinkle the crushed pistachios and freeze-dried raspberries on the frosting, if desired. The mini cakes (without foliage) keep covered in the refrigerator for up to 3 days. Remove the cakes 1 to 2 hours before serving, so the frosting has time to soften.

How to
DECORATE CAKES

People often ask me where the idea to decorate cakes with flowers came from. The truth is, it started during COVID, when I found myself missing home—especially my mother's cakes and her garden. Sometimes, she'd place roses on her cakes, and the combination of the cake's aroma with the scent of fresh flowers is a memory I hold close.

Although I had a foundation thanks to my mum, I've since taken the time to learn more about which flowers are safe to use with food and how to use others I love in a safe way. Over the years, I've also embraced working seasonally, not just with flavors but with flowers, too. It's a process that teaches you to pay attention to the rhythms of the world around you and find inspiration in what's naturally available. The result is decorations that evolve with the changing seasons. To guide you in creating your own, I've provided a list of seasonal flowers and greenery that offer flexibility and variety, ensuring you have plenty of options to work with throughout the year.

While I use a mix of flower sizes on most of my cakes, when decorating mini cakes and sheet cakes, I usually stick to smaller blooms. To round out my cake decorations, I often use slices of dehydrated fruit, as well as crushed unsalted and unroasted pistachios and freeze-dried raspberries. They add a beautiful texture and an earthy, vibrant touch that brings the entire cake together. For some cakes, I also add Meringue Letters (page 71) or numbers, which are a fun way to celebrate a birthday or other special occasion. Each cake is unique, but here's the basic step-by-step process.

1. Pick seasonal flowers and greenery for decorating your cake. (Keep them in a vase of water in the fridge until ready to use.)

2. Always rinse flowers and greenery before using them.

3. Envision where you're going to place your flowers and greenery on the cake, how long you want the stems to be, and whether you want them to be vertical or at an angle.

4. Cut the stems depending on whether you are using floral tape or floral water tubes and how much dimension you want to create on the cake.

5. Wrap the ends of your stems in floral tape or put them in floral water tubes as needed.

6. Introduce the flowers and greenery into your cake. If using tape or water tubes, push the flowers far enough into the cake to make the tube or tape flush with the top of the buttercream.

7. Use buttercream to fill in any gaps and hide any floral tape or floral water tubes.

8. Add smaller flowers and greenery for additional camouflage, as well as to give your cake more dimension.

9. Fill in any remaining gaps with a few dehydrated fruit slices, then sprinkle the crushed pistachios and freeze-dried raspberries on the buttercream. (Crush the pistachios using a food processor or mortar and pestle but use your hands to crush the freeze-dried raspberries; you want both to be a mix of powder and small crumbs.)

10. If using Meringue Letters (page 71) on a tiered cake, pipe a small dollop of buttercream on the flat part of the middle tier and a small dollop on the vertical wall or side of the top tier. Carefully arrange the meringue letter in place and gently wiggle, so it's secure and doesn't move. Repeat with additional letters as needed. If you are using meringue letters on a standard layer cake or a sheet cake, simply lay them on top, but again, be gentle!

CHOOSING FLOWERS AND GREENERY

When it comes to decorating cakes with flowers, I always strive to work with the most natural blooms. That's why I recommend choosing pesticide-free, organic flowers whenever possible. I've developed a way of categorizing flowers into three distinct groups to guide my decisions:

EDIBLE FLOWERS

They are perfect for adding delicate, smaller decorations that enhance both the beauty and flavor of cakes. However, when I say "edible flowers," I don't mean you can consume the whole plant—stems, leaves, and all. If you're eating the flower, discard the greens and keep the bloom. Some blooms, like cornflowers or chamomile, can be enjoyed in their entirety. Others, such as roses, scabiosas, or orchids, are best when only the petals are consumed.

NONTOXIC FLOWERS

While safe to ingest, they don't offer much flavor, so they're best suited for decorating purposes.

TOXIC FLOWERS

As their name implies, these should never be eaten. However, they can still be used to enhance the design of a cake, as long as the proper precautions are taken (see page 85).

When it comes to greenery, you can use fresh herbs, or simply foliage, as long as the pieces are sturdy and can hold their shape long enough. Make sure the scent of your greenery doesn't overpower your cake; plants like eucalyptus can have a very powerful aroma.

TIPS FOR WORKING WITH FLOWERS

More often than not, flowers are used purely for decoration and removed before the cake is served, which allows us to choose from a wider selection of blooms. However, there are some important tips to follow to ensure flowers are both beautiful and safe.

1. When purchasing flowers, it's best to buy them slightly closed (unbloomed) and open them up yourself. This helps them last longer and reduces the chance of petals shedding prematurely. One way to open flowers is to hold the stem between both hands, then gently tip the flower upside down and rub your hands together quickly to help open the petals. Another technique involves using your thumb to gently push the outer petals away from the center, working your way inward without tearing the petals. This lets you shape flowers exactly how you like. For peonies, I prefer dipping them in warm water for a few seconds to encourage the blooms to relax and open. If you purchase flowers in advance, keep them in the fridge so they stay fresh until you're ready to use them.

2. One of my favorite things to do is visit my local florist or flower grower and ask if they have any flowers with stems that are broken or too short for a bouquet. These flowers are often perfect for cakes and buying them helps reduce waste. I also seek out flowers that are older, wilted, or otherwise imperfect. You can collect the petals that still look good and stamp them onto cakes as another decoration.

3. Always rinse flowers thoroughly to remove any dirt or bugs from organic flowers, and as much pesticide residue as possible from nonorganic flowers. Rinse sturdier petals in water directly from the sink's faucet. Dip more delicate flowers upside down in a bowl of water. Lightly blot the blossoms on a paper towel, then let them dry completely before using. Greenery can be washed under the sink, but carefully wipe down the leaves with a paper towel to make them shiny and prevent water spots.

4. Depending on your decorating and serving plans, you may want to use floral tape or floral water tubes to introduce the flowers into the cake. Floral tape is best when you're serving the cake within a couple of hours. If you won't be serving the cake for longer than a couple of hours, or if you're working with flowers that wilt or die quickly, I highly recommend using floral water tubes, which will keep the blooms fresh longer.

Floral tubes are also crucial for flowers with stems that release a lot of sap, as they help prevent the sap from leaking into the cake, and when working with toxic flowers. I've had clients request specific flowers that are toxic, and in those cases, it's essential to ensure the flower and its stem never touch the cake—only the floral tube should come in contact with the cake. Another time to use floral tubes is when working with dahlias, marigolds, or any flower that has an unpleasant smell when the stem is cut—the tube keeps the scent out of your cake. Be cautious with the number of floral tubes you use, as they can take up space and make the cake more fragile, so use them mostly for delicate flowers that won't last as long out of water.

Smaller flowers don't have sap, so if they are edible or nontoxic, you can insert the stems directly into the cake. But if a small flower is toxic, be sure to wrap the stem in floral tape before introducing it into the cake.

5. I always try to work with the natural shape and length of flowers and their stems to create a more dynamic, layered effect on cakes. For instance, flowers like scabiosas, tulips, and ranunculus have beautiful, wavy stems that lend themselves to being left long and arranged so they extend dramatically from the cake. In contrast, flowers like roses, peonies, and chrysanthemums have more rigid, straight stems, and they look best when the bloom is close to the cake. Arranging some flowers close to the cake and others so there is some distance between the cake and the bloom, and so the stems are visible, helps create visual interest. Another way to create dimension is to arrange your flowers so that some are vertical, and some are at an angle—I aim for a roughly 45-degree angle. I also love incorporating greenery and smaller flowers to add texture and fill in any gaps.

6. Ideally, you're putting the flowers on just before serving, but if you are adding the flowers ahead, keep the cake in the fridge.

LARGE AND SMALL FLOWERS AND GREENERY FOR DECORATING

SMALL FLOWERS

Blue borage blossom (edible)

Butterfly ranunculus (toxic, only to be used safely)

Chamomile flower (edible)

Chive flower (edible)

Coral charm heirloom chrysanthemum (edible)

Cornflower (edible)

Cosmos (edible)

Cushion chrysanthemum (edible)

Geraldton waxflower (edible)

Grape hyacinth bulb (edible)

Lilac (edible)

Lisianthus (not edible)

Micro star flower / princess flower (edible)

Nasturtium (edible)

Scabiosa (edible)

Spray rose (edible)

Strawflower (not edible)

LARGE FLOWERS

Allium (edible)

Chrysanthemum (edible)

Dahlia (edible)

Dried amaranth (edible)

Marigold (edible)

Orchid (edible)

Queen Anne's lace (edible)

Peony (edible)

Ranunculus (toxic, only to be used safely)

Rose (edible)

Snapdragon (edible)

Tulip (edible, except the core)

GREENERY

Browned maple leaf (for decoration only)

Dahlia bulb, closed (for decoration only)

Jasmine vine (for decoration only)

Nandina (for decoration only)

Rosemary (edible)

Peppergrass (edible)

Smilax (for decoration only)

Spray rose bulb, closed (for decoration only)

Thyme (edible)

PIÈCE DE RÉSISTANCE

Showstopping Cakes

RASPBERRY YOGURT BASIL CAKE

MAKES ONE 8-INCH / 20CM TWO-LAYER CAKE

Yogurt cake is a French classic. It's very light and can be served on its own, with perhaps a dollop of crème fraîche, or as shown here (and my sister-in-law's favorite version), studded with raspberries and finished with a Swiss meringue buttercream that's been infused with basil, plus raspberry jam spread between the layers and spooned on top.

Flavoring the buttercream with basil is a clin d'oeil (wink) to the basil my mother grows in wine barrels right below her kitchen window. On hot summer days, when making pâtes au pistou (pesto pasta), she simply opens the shutters, cuts a few stems, et voilà—fresh basil without even going outside.

To keep this recipe manageable, I recommend making the jam and the basil-infused butter a day or so ahead—you can also use store-bought jam to skip a step.

RASPBERRY YOGURT CAKE

- Canola oil spray or canola oil, for the pans
- 2½ cups / 350g all-purpose flour
- 1½ teaspoons baking powder
- ½ teaspoon baking soda
- ½ teaspoon fine sea salt
- 2 sticks plus 2 tablespoons / 256g unsalted butter, at room temperature and cut into small pieces
- 2 cups / 400g sugar
- 3 large eggs, at room temperature
- 1 cup / 240g whole-milk yogurt (not Greek), at room temperature
- 1 teaspoon vanilla extract
- 1 teaspoon grated lemon zest (from 1 medium lemon)
- 2 cups / 240g raspberries, fresh or frozen (not thawed)

BASIL SWISS MERINGUE BUTTERCREAM

- Distilled white vinegar
- 140g egg whites (about 4 large), at room temperature
- 1 cup / 200g sugar
- 2 sticks plus 2 tablespoons / 256g unsalted butter, at cool room temperature and cut into small pieces
- 6 tablespoons / 90g Basil-Infused Butter (recipe follows), at cool room temperature and cut into small pieces
- ⅛ teaspoon fine sea salt

ASSEMBLY

- About ½ cup / 150g raspberry jam, homemade (recipe follows) or store-bought
- Large and small flowers and greenery (see page 88), for decorating
- Dehydrated fruit slices (page 103), crushed pistachios (page 83), and crushed freeze-dried raspberries (page 83), for decorating (optional)

1. FOR THE RASPBERRY YOGURT CAKE: Set a rack in the middle of the oven and preheat to 350°F / 180°C. Spray or brush the sides of two 8-inch / 20cm round cake pans with canola oil, then line the bottoms with parchment paper.

2. Sift the flour, baking powder, and baking soda into a medium bowl. Add the salt.

3. In a stand mixer fitted with the paddle, beat the butter and sugar on medium speed, scraping down the bottom and sides of the bowl as needed, until pale and fluffy, about 4 minutes. Scrape the bowl, then beat on high speed for 1 minute more. Scrape the bowl, then add the eggs, one at a time, and beat on medium-low speed, scraping the bowl before each addition and again at the end, until fully incorporated. Add the yogurt, vanilla, and lemon zest and beat on low speed until fully incorporated, about 30 seconds. Add the flour mixture in four batches and mix, scraping the bowl before each addition, just until there are no streaks. Do not overmix! Scrape the bowl one final time to make sure the flour is fully incorporated.

4. Divide the batter evenly between the prepared pans, smoothing the tops. Dividing the raspberries evenly, use your fingers to poke them into the batter. I like to put them about ½ inch / 13mm apart, with a few along the edges, so raspberries pop out on the sides of the baked cakes.

RECIPE CONTINUES

5. Bake for 20 minutes, then quickly rotate the pans and continue baking until the cakes are lightly golden on top and spring back when lightly pressed, 15 to 20 minutes.

6. Let the cakes cool in the pans on a wire rack for 20 minutes. Carefully run a small offset spatula between the edges of the pans and the cakes, then flip the pans onto the rack and tap them to make sure the cakes are released. Remove the parchment paper. Use a second rack or a plate to flip the cakes so they are right-side up on the rack. Let cool completely.

7. **FOR THE BASIL SWISS MERINGUE BUTTERCREAM:** (Before starting, read How to Make Swiss Meringue Buttercream, page 129.) Fill a medium saucepan with about 1 inch / 2.5cm of water and bring to a simmer over medium-low heat.

8. Use a paper towel and about ¼ teaspoon of white vinegar to wipe all over the surface of a large heatproof bowl and the bowl of a stand mixer, making sure there aren't any traces of liquid or fat.

9. In the clean heatproof bowl, combine the egg whites and sugar, then set the bowl over the pan of simmering water, making sure the water does not touch the bottom of the bowl. Heat the mixture, whisking constantly, until it registers 130°F / 54°C on an instant-read thermometer, 3 to 4 minutes.

10. Transfer the mixture to the clean bowl of the stand mixer. Using the whisk attachment, whip on high speed until stiff peaks form, 8 to 10 minutes. Switch to the paddle attachment. Gradually start adding the plain butter and basil-infused butter in small batches and beat on medium-high speed, scraping the bowl as needed, until all the butter has been added. Beat on high speed until the buttercream is fluffy and has air bubbles, about 1 minute. Add the salt and beat on low speed until fully incorporated, about 30 seconds.

11. **TO ASSEMBLE:** Place a cake layer, flat-side down, on a cake plate or stand.

12. Put about 2 cups / 330g of the buttercream into a piping bag fitted with a plain round tip with a ½-inch / 13mm or similar diameter. Holding the pastry tip about 1 inch / 2.5cm above the cake and starting about ¼ inch / 6mm from the edge, pipe 2 concentric rounded rings of buttercream around the perimeter. Spoon the raspberry jam into the middle and use a small offset spatula to spread it evenly. Pipe zigzags of buttercream on top of the jam so it's completely covered. Using a small offset spatula, gently spread the buttercream zigzags to fill in any gaps and connect them to the outer rings of buttercream, while leaving them intact.

13. Carefully place the second cake layer, flat-side up, on top, then gently wiggle it into the buttercream. Add more buttercream to the piping bag as needed.

14. Repeat the above process but pipe a single ring on the very edge of the cake and skip the jam. Once the top is covered in buttercream, use the tip of a small offset spatula to create some swooshes and texture on top of the cake (see How to Assemble, Frost, and Cut a Layer Cake, page 53).

15. Arrange a few large and small flowers and greenery on top of the cake (see Tips for Working with Flowers, page 85). Add the dehydrated fruit slices and sprinkle the pistachios and freeze-dried raspberries on the buttercream, if desired. The cake (without foliage) keeps covered in the refrigerator for up to 2 days. Remove the cake about 2 hours before serving, so the buttercream has time to soften.

Basil-Infused Butter

MAKES ⅔ CUP / 150G

1 stick plus 4 tablespoons / 168g unsalted butter, cut into small pieces
2 tablespoons tightly packed fresh basil leaves, roughly chopped

1. In a small saucepan, melt the butter over medium-low heat. Remove from the heat, then stir in the basil, cover, and let stand for 30 minutes.

2. Pour through a fine-mesh sieve set over a medium bowl, pressing on the basil to extract as much flavor as possible (discard the basil). Cover and refrigerate, stirring every 20 minutes, until the butter starts to firm up, about 1 hour, then leave it alone to chill completely, at least 1 hour and up to 1 week. The butter can also be well wrapped and frozen for up to 2 months; thaw in the refrigerator overnight.

Raspberry Jam

MAKES 4 CUPS / 1.2KG

3 pounds / 1.4kg raspberries (about 11½ cups), fresh or thawed frozen
4 cups / 800g sugar
1 teaspoon fine sea salt
Juice of 2 lemons

1. Put two small plates in the freezer.

2. In a large Dutch oven or heavy-bottomed saucepan, combine the raspberries and sugar and cook over medium-high heat, stirring frequently to keep the fruit from burning. As the mixture comes to a boil, use a large stainless steel spoon to skim off the light pink foam that rises to the top.

3. When the jam starts to feel a bit thick, scoop a spoonful onto one of the frozen plates and wait 1 to 2 minutes for it to come to room temperature. Tip the plate from side to side. If the jam is ready, it will hold its shape on the plate rather than run down it. If you're not sure, try running a spoon through the jam on the plate—if it holds the line, it's ready. Technically, jam should register about 220°F / 104°C, and if you're new to jam making, using a thermometer can be really helpful, but part of the fun is relying on your senses. The jam should have a smooth texture studded with raspberry seeds but no chunks of fruit. If needed, continue cooking the jam until it sets on the second frozen plate.

4. Once the jam passes the plate test, add the salt and lemon juice, then remove it from the heat. If you want to seal the jam in jars for longer term storage, do so while it's still hot (see How to Can Jams and Curds, page 187).

5. Otherwise, let the jam stand in the pot, without stirring, to cool and thicken for about 30 minutes, then transfer it to jars or airtight containers but do not cover. Let the jam cool to room temperature, then cover and refrigerate for up to 2 weeks. You can cool the jam in the refrigerator, but it's important to allow the jam to fully cool before covering, as condensation could drip back into your beautiful work and loosen the texture.

RED WINE CHOCOLATE PEAR GINGER DOME CAKE

MAKES ONE 8-INCH / 20CM DOME CAKE

This cake holds a special place in my heart. Growing up on a vineyard in France, I spent my school holidays working in the vines to make pocket money, surrounded by my father's winemaking passion. At age eleven, I started learning about wine and the complexities of different flavor notes. As a result, I have a deep love for pairing food with wine, so naturally, I had to create a cake using my family's wine. Infused with a rich, full-bodied red wine, the cake is paired with a velvety chocolate ginger mousseline buttercream and pear ginger jam—my love for red wine–poached pears definitely inspired this cake. The buttercream can seem intimidating at first, but once you've nailed making a custard, you'll be able to make it blindfolded. For the pear ginger jam, I like to leave bits of pear in the mix to preserve the texture.

RED WINE DOME CAKE

Canola oil spray or canola oil, for the pan
2½ cups / 350g all-purpose flour
2½ teaspoons baking soda
½ cup plus 1 tablespoon / 135g sour cream, at room temperature
2 large eggs, at room temperature
1 tablespoon vanilla extract
2 sticks plus 2 tablespoons / 256g unsalted butter, cut into small pieces
1 cup / 240ml red wine, such as Cabernet Sauvignon or Merlot
2 cups / 400g granulated sugar
2 tablespoons unsweetened Dutch-process cocoa powder

CHOCOLATE GINGER MOUSSELINE BUTTERCREAM

5 large egg yolks, at room temperature
¼ cup / 30g cornstarch
½ cup / 100g granulated sugar
2 cups / 480ml whole milk
1 teaspoon vanilla extract
5 ounces / 140g dark chocolate
3 sticks / 339g unsalted butter, at room temperature and cut into small pieces
½ cup / 60g powdered sugar, sifted
⅓ cup / 25g unsweetened Dutch-process cocoa powder
2 teaspoons ground ginger

ASSEMBLY

About 1 cup / 390g Pear Ginger Jam (recipe follows)
Sugared grapes (page 104), for decorating

1. FOR THE RED WINE DOME CAKE: Set a rack in the middle of the oven and preheat to 350°F / 180°C. Spray or brush the sides of a 1½-quart/1.4L stainless steel bowl with an 8-inch / 20cm diameter opening with canola oil, then line the base with a round of parchment paper.

2. Sift the flour and baking soda into a medium bowl.

3. In a small bowl, whisk together the sour cream, eggs, and vanilla.

4. In a large saucepan, combine the butter and red wine and warm over medium heat until the butter is melted. Remove from the heat, then add the granulated sugar and cocoa powder and whisk until smooth. Add the sour cream mixture and whisk until fully combined. Gradually add the flour mixture, whisking until smooth.

5. Pour the batter into the prepared bowl and bake until a skewer inserted in the center of the cake comes out clean, about 1 hour 15 minutes.

6. Set the bowl on a wire rack and let cool for 30 minutes. Flip the bowl over to release the cake, then remove the parchment paper and let the cake cool completely.

7. FOR THE CHOCOLATE GINGER MOUSSELINE BUTTERCREAM: In a large bowl, combine the egg yolks, cornstarch, and 2 tablespoons of the granulated sugar and whisk until fully combined and smooth.

8. In a small saucepan, combine the milk, vanilla, and the remaining 6 tablespoons / 90g granulated sugar and heat over medium-low heat until warm. While whisking continuously, gradually add the warm milk mixture to the egg yolk mixture. Pour this mixture back into the

RECIPE CONTINUES

saucepan and cook, whisking continuously, until it has a thick custard-like consistency, about 3 minutes. Pour through a fine-mesh sieve set over a medium bowl. Cover with plastic wrap, pressing the plastic wrap directly onto the surface of the custard to prevent a skin from forming, and refrigerate until cold, about 2 hours.

9. When the custard is cold, fill a medium saucepan with about 1 inch / 2.5cm of water and bring to a simmer over medium-low heat. Add the dark chocolate to a large heatproof bowl, then set the bowl over the pan of simmering water, making sure the water does not touch the bottom of the bowl. Warm the chocolate, stirring occasionally, until melted. Remove the bowl from the pan (careful—it will be warm!) and use a clean kitchen towel to carefully wipe any condensation from the bottom of the bowl. Let the chocolate cool slightly.

10. In a stand mixer fitted with the paddle, beat the butter and powdered sugar on medium speed for 1 minute, then increase the speed to high and beat until light and fluffy, about 3 minutes. Scrape down the bottom and sides of the bowl, then add the cocoa powder and ground ginger and mix on low speed until fully incorporated, about 30 seconds. On medium-low speed, gradually mix in the cooled custard, 1 tablespoon at a time, until fully incorporated. Add the cooled chocolate and beat on medium speed until the chocolate is incorporated and the buttercream is smooth and silky.

11. TO ASSEMBLE: Using a serrated knife, cut the cake horizontally into three even layers. Place the wide bottom layer, flat-side down, on a cake plate.

12. Put about 2 cups / 400g of the buttercream into a piping bag fitted with a plain round tip with a ½-inch / 13mm or similar diameter. Holding the pastry tip about 1 inch / 2.5cm above the cake and starting about ¼ inch / 6mm from the edge, pipe 2 concentric rounded rings of buttercream around the perimeter. Spoon about ½ cup / 195g of the pear ginger jam into the middle and use a small offset spatula to spread it evenly. Pipe zigzags of buttercream on top of the jam so it's completely covered. Using a small offset spatula, gently spread the buttercream zigzags to fill in any gaps and connect them to the outer rings.

13. Carefully place the second cake layer, wider-side down on top, then gently wiggle it into the buttercream. Add more buttercream to the piping bag as needed.

14. Repeat the above process to pipe and spread the buttercream and add the jam to the second cake layer.

15. Place the final layer (or dome), flat-side down, on top, then gently wiggle it into the buttercream. Using a small offset spatula, spread the buttercream in a thin, even layer to completely cover the outside of the cake. This is your crumb coat. You should still be able to see some of the cake underneath. Put the cake in the refrigerator for 15 minutes to firm up. (See How to Assemble, Frost, and Cut a Layer Cake, page 53.)

16. Add the remaining buttercream to a piping bag fitted with a small open star tip, then pipe vertical stripes of buttercream from the bottom to the top of the cake. Decorate the top with swirls of buttercream, then place a cluster of sugared grapes in the center. Arrange individual sugared grapes around the base of the cake for a finished look. The cake is best the day it's made, but it keeps covered in the refrigerator for up to 2 days. Remove the cake about 2 hours before serving, so the buttercream has time to soften.

Pear Ginger Jam

MAKES 4 CUPS / 1.5KG

7 pounds / 3.2kg ripe fresh pears (about 16 medium pears), peeled, cored, and cut into small cubes
4½ cups / 900g sugar
2 tablespoons vanilla bean paste
2 teaspoons ground ginger
2 teaspoons freshly squeezed lemon juice (from 1 medium lemon)
¼ teaspoon fine sea salt

1. In a medium bowl, toss the pear cubes and sugar together to coat the fruit. Cover and let macerate for 2 hours at room temperature or preferably overnight in the refrigerator.

2. When ready to make the jam, put two small plates in the freezer.

3. Add the macerated pears to a large Dutch oven or heavy-bottomed saucepan. Set over medium heat and cook, stirring frequently and mashing the pears against the side of the pan if you want the jam to be smooth, until the pears are quite mushy, 20 to 25 minutes.

4. Continue cooking and stirring until the pears are fully broken down and the jam is thick, 5 to 8 minutes more. Scoop a spoonful onto one of the frozen plates and wait 1 to 2 minutes for it to come to room temperature. Tip the plate from side to side. If the jam is ready, it will hold its shape on the plate rather than run down it. If you're not sure, try running a spoon through the jam on the plate—if it holds the line, it's ready. Technically, jam should register about 220°F / 104°C, and if you're new to jam making, using a thermometer can be really helpful, but part of the fun is relying on your senses. The jam will be syrupy with chunks of pear, unless you mashed the fruit while cooking to make it thicker and smoother. If needed, continue cooking the jam until it sets on the second frozen plate.

5. Once the jam passes the frozen plate test, stir in the vanilla bean paste, ginger, lemon juice, and salt, then remove it from the heat. If you want to seal the jam in jars for longer term storage, do so while it's still hot (see How to Can Jams and Curds, page 187).

6. Otherwise, let the jam stand in the pot, without stirring, to cool and thicken for about 30 minutes, then transfer it to jars or airtight containers but do not cover. Let the jam cool to room temperature, then cover and refrigerate for up to 2 weeks. You can cool the jam in the refrigerator, but it's important to allow the jam to fully cool before covering, as condensation could drip back into your beautiful work and loosen the texture.

How to
DEHYDRATE AND SUGAR FRUIT

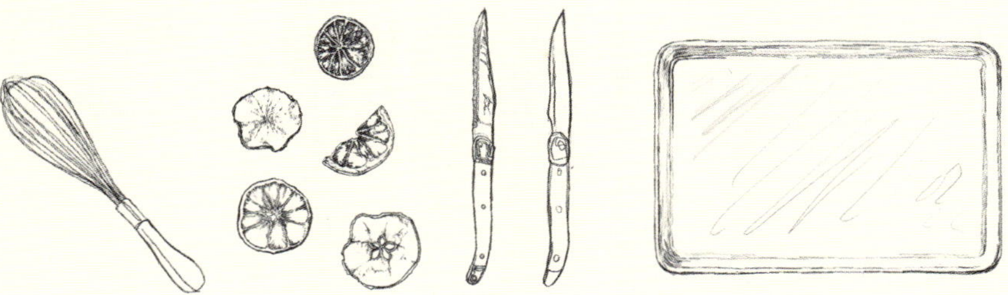

Dehydrating and sugaring are simple yet effective ways to make the most of fruit—whether you're looking to intensify its flavor (dehydrating) or give it a touch of frosted glam (sugaring)—and add a little extra decoration to cakes. Dehydrating brings out fruit's natural sweetness and adds a satisfying bit of crunch, while sugaring lends a beautifully wintry look with just the right amount of sweetness. I always seem to have a mound of extra fruit, and both these methods are a handy way to put it to good use. Here are a few little tricks to help you get the best results every time.

DEHYDRATED FRUIT SLICES

You can easily dehydrate fruit at home, even without a dehydrator. All you need is a sharp knife, a baking sheet, and an oven.

I like to work with citrus fruit, apples, and pears, as they hold their structure best when dehydrated, but feel free to try this method with any fruit you desire. Look for fruit that is fresh, ripe, and with even color; avoid mushy or stained fruit. Keep in mind that the fruit will shrink in the dehydrating process, so you may want to make more than you think you need.

1. Set a rack in the middle of the oven and preheat to 200°F / 90°C. Line a baking sheet with parchment paper.

2. Wash and dry the fruit thoroughly, then remove any inedible peels and cut into slices ⅛ to ¼ inch / 3 to 6mm thick.

3. To minimize browning, lightly spritz the fruit slices with lemon juice.

4. Arrange the fruit slices in a single layer, making sure they don't overlap.

5. Bake the fruit, flipping it every hour, until stiff and crunchy, 6 to 9 hours, depending on the fruit and the thickness. Dehydrated fruit can be stored in an airtight container at room temperature for up to 2 weeks, but it may not last that long if it's humid outside.

SUGARED FRUIT

While you need only a few ingredients to sugar fruit, it's important to use the right sugar or the fruit won't look quite as nice. Quick-dissolve superfine sugar, aka caster sugar, is easy to find in Europe, but for some reason harder to source in the US. If you can't find it, simply put granulated sugar in a blender and pulse it until it has a finer texture.

Sugared fruits are best the day they are made, as the sugar will soften and turn wet if the fruit is put in the refrigerator. But plan ahead so there's ample time for the sugar to set and harden before you use the fruit to decorate.

Only whole fruit can be sugared—no slices or chunks—and it's best to use fruit that's still a bit firm rather than too ripe. Ideally, this means grapes and berries. Before sugaring berries, make sure they are completely dry, as they tend to trap water. Strawberries contain a lot of water, so they're not ideal for sugaring. Stick to blueberries, blackberries, and raspberries.

You can also sugar flowers, as long as they're organic, as well as herbs, such as rosemary.

The following proportions are based on 3 cups / 360 to 420g of berries:

1. Line the bottom of a baking sheet with parchment paper, then set a wire rack inside the baking sheet.

2. Add 2 large room temperature egg whites to a medium bowl and whisk them slightly. Add ½ cup / 100g superfine sugar to a second medium bowl.

3. Using a pastry brush, coat 3 cups / 360 to 420g fresh berries with the egg whites. (Don't drop the fruit in the bowl of egg whites, as you don't want too much on the fruit.) Working in small batches, drop the coated berries in the sugar and use a small spoon to gently roll them to fully cover them in sugar.

4. Set the berries on the wire rack and let dry until the sugar is firm, 15 to 30 minutes, depending on the humidity in the air.

NET WT 5 LBS (2.27kg)
CREAM

VEGAN LEMON ELDERFLOWER CAKE

MAKES ONE 8-INCH / 20CM TWO-LAYER CAKE

Incredibly moist and zesty, this was one of the first recipes I developed for the bakery because I kept getting requests for vegan cakes. To create a bright yellow curd without any eggs, I add a touch of turmeric. I pair the curd with lemon sponge and elderflower frosting, a classic combination that should stay that way! It's tempting to use different plant-based milks, but I find soy milk produces the best structure and texture for both the sponge and the frosting. The recipe includes a range for how much soy milk to use in the frosting, so you can experiment with how soft or stiff you make it. In the summer, when the kitchen is warm, I usually need to use a bit less.

LEMON CAKE

Canola oil spray or canola oil, for the pans
2½ cups / 350g all-purpose flour
1½ teaspoons baking soda
1½ cups / 300g granulated sugar
1 teaspoon fine sea salt
1⅓ cups plus 1 tablespoon / 335ml soy milk
½ cup plus 2 tablespoons / 150ml canola oil
1 tablespoon apple cider vinegar
1 teaspoon vanilla extract
3 tablespoons grated lemon zest (from 3 medium lemons)

ELDERFLOWER FROSTING

1 stick plus 6 tablespoons / 198g plant-based butter, at room temperature and cut into small pieces
6 cups / 720g powdered sugar, sifted
3 to 5 tablespoons / 45 to 75ml soy milk, at room temperature
3 tablespoons elderflower syrup
½ teaspoon fine sea salt

ASSEMBLY

About ½ cup / 130g Vegan Lemon Curd (recipe follows)
Large and small flowers and greenery (see page 88), for decorating

1. FOR THE LEMON CAKE: Set a rack in the middle of the oven and preheat to 325°F / 160°C. Spray or brush the bottom and sides of two 8-inch / 20cm round cake pans with canola oil, then line the bottoms with parchment paper.

2. Sift the flour and baking soda into a medium bowl. Add the granulated sugar and salt and whisk to combine.

3. In a large bowl, whisk together the soy milk, canola oil, vinegar, and vanilla. Add the flour mixture in three additions and whisk until there are no lumps. Add the lemon zest and fold with a rubber spatula until incorporated.

4. Divide the batter evenly between the prepared pans and bake for 15 minutes, then quickly rotate the pans and bake until the cakes spring back when lightly pressed, about 15 minutes.

5. Let the cakes cool in the pans on a wire rack for 20 minutes. Carefully run a small offset spatula between the edges of the pans and the cakes, then flip the pans onto the rack and tap them to make sure the cakes are released. Remove the parchment paper. Use a second rack or a plate to flip the cakes so they are right-side up on the rack. Let cool completely.

6. FOR THE ELDERFLOWER FROSTING: In a stand mixer fitted with the paddle, beat the plant-based butter on medium-high speed, scraping down the bottom and sides of the bowl as needed, until creamy and lighter in color, about 3 minutes. Scrape the bowl, then add 1 cup / 120g of the powdered sugar and beat on low speed for 15 seconds. Increase the speed to medium and beat until fully incorporated, about 15 seconds. Repeat the process 5 times, scraping the bowl before each addition and again at the end, until fully incorporated. Add 3 tablespoons of the soy milk, along with the elderflower syrup and salt, and beat for 1 minute. Increase the speed to high and beat until fluffy and easily spreadable, about 2 minutes. If the frosting is too stiff, add more soy milk, 1 tablespoon at a time, until spreadable.

7. TO ASSEMBLE: Place a cake layer, flat-side down, on a cake plate or stand.

RECIPE CONTINUES

8. Put about 2 cups / 520g of the frosting into a piping bag fitted with a plain round tip with a ½-inch / 13mm or similar diameter.

9. Holding the pastry tip about 1 inch / 2.5cm above the cake and starting about ½ inch / 13mm from the edge, pipe 2 concentric rounded rings of frosting around the perimeter. Spoon the lemon curd into the middle and use a small offset spatula to spread it evenly. Pipe zigzags of frosting on top of the curd so it's completely covered. Using a small offset spatula, gently spread the frosting zigzags to fill in any gaps and connect them to the outer rings of frosting, while leaving them intact.

10. Carefully place the second cake layer, flat-side up, on top, then gently wiggle it into the frosting. Add more frosting to the piping bag as needed.

11. Repeat the above process but pipe a single ring on the very edge of the cake and skip the curd. Once the top is covered in buttercream, use the tip of a small offset spatula to create some swooshes and texture on top of the cake (see How to Assemble, Frost, and Cut a Layer Cake, page 53).

12. Holding the pastry tip about 1 inch / 2.5cm above the cake, pipe 4 large dollops of buttercream along the outside edge of the cake. Dip a teaspoon in hot water, then use it to create divots or "bowls" in each dollop of buttercream. Use two small spoons to plop some curd in each buttercream "bowl."

13. Arrange a few large flowers and greenery on top of the cake, then fill in any remaining gaps with small flowers (see Tips for Working with Flowers, page 85). The cake (without foliage) keeps covered in the refrigerator for up to 4 days. Remove the cake about 1 hour before serving, so the frosting has time to soften.

Vegan Lemon Curd

MAKES ABOUT 2 CUPS / 520G

1 cup plus 2 tablespoons / 270ml soy milk
1 cup / 200g sugar
3 tablespoons cornstarch
8 teaspoons grated lemon zest (from 3 medium lemons)
½ cup / 120ml freshly squeezed lemon juice (from 3 medium lemons)
¼ teaspoon ground turmeric

1. In a medium saucepan, combine the soy milk, sugar, cornstarch, lemon zest, and lemon juice. Cook the mixture over medium heat, whisking constantly, until the sugar is dissolved and the curd just starts to thicken, about 4 minutes. Add the turmeric and continue cooking, stirring occasionally with a rubber spatula, until the curd thickens and starts to bubble, 2 to 3 minutes. The curd should turn yellow at this point.

2. Pour the mixture into a small bowl, then press a piece of plastic wrap directly onto the surface of the curd to prevent a skin from forming. Refrigerate until the curd is cold and thick, 1 to 1½ hours. The curd keeps in an airtight container in the refrigerator for up to 5 days. If the curd separates in the fridge, whisk it to bring it back together before using.

ALL-PURPOSE
BROWNED BUTTER AT
3.30

PEAR RASPBERRY BROWN BUTTER MAPLE SHEET CAKE

MAKES ONE 9 × 13-INCH / 23 × 33CM TWO-LAYER SHEET CAKE

This is my go-to fall cake. The second I see leaves turning orange, I'm eating oatmeal topped with pears, raspberry jam, and maple syrup for breakfast, so why not turn this combo into a cake? I even had the privilege of making this cake alongside Martha Stewart on her show—so you know it's Martha-approved!

Using almond flour and brown sugar in the sponge enhances the warmth of this soft and buttery cake, while chunks of pear lend sweetness, and raspberries bring tartness. The brown butter in the buttercream draws out the nuttiness of the maple syrup, and it can be made ahead to make life a bit easier. For an extra touch, I love to dehydrate a few extra pears to decorate the top of the cake (see How to Dehydrate and Sugar Fruit, page 103).

PEAR RASPBERRY CAKE

Canola oil spray or canola oil, for the pans
2¾ cups / 385g all-purpose flour
2¼ teaspoons baking powder
1½ teaspoons baking soda
1 cup / 100g almond flour
½ teaspoon fine sea salt
3 sticks / 339g unsalted butter, at room temperature and cut into small pieces
1½ cups / 300g (packed) light brown sugar
1 teaspoon grated orange zest (from 1 medium orange)
1½ teaspoons vanilla extract
4 large eggs, at room temperature
1⅓ cups / 320g sour cream, at room temperature
1⅔ cups / 200g fresh raspberries
1 medium pear (about 7 ounces / 200g), unpeeled and cut into ½-inch / 13mm pieces

BROWN BUTTER MAPLE BUTTERCREAM

8 sticks plus 2 tablespoons / 935g unsalted butter, at room temperature and cut into small pieces
7½ cups / 900g powdered sugar, sifted
1 cup plus 2 tablespoons / 270ml maple syrup
4 teaspoons vanilla extract
2 teaspoons fine sea salt
1 teaspoon grated orange zest (from 1 medium orange)

ASSEMBLY

About 1½ cups / 450g raspberry jam, homemade (page 95) or store-bought
Small flowers and greenery (see page 88), for decorating
Dehydrated fruit slices (page 103), crushed pistachios (page 83), and crushed freeze-dried raspberries (page 83), for decorating (optional)

1. FOR THE PEAR RASPBERRY CAKE: Set a rack in the middle of the oven and preheat to 350°F / 180°C. Spray or brush the bottom and sides of two 9 × 13-inch / 23 × 33cm or similarly sized baking sheets with canola oil and line the bottoms with parchment paper.

2. Sift the flour, baking powder, and baking soda into a large bowl. Add the almond flour and salt.

3. In a stand mixer fitted with the paddle, beat the butter on medium-high speed until pale and smooth, about 3 minutes. Scrape down the bottom and sides of the bowl, then add the brown sugar, orange zest, and vanilla and beat until thick and creamy, about 2 minutes. Scrape the bowl, then add the eggs, one at a time, and beat, scraping the bowl before each addition and again at the end, until fully incorporated.

4. Beat for 30 seconds more, or until pale and slightly fluffy, then scrape the bowl. Add the flour mixture in three batches and mix on low speed, scraping the bowl before each addition, just until there are no streaks. Scrape the bowl, then add the sour cream and mix on medium speed just until there are no streaks, about 30 seconds. The batter will be thick.

5. Carefully divide the batter between the two prepared pans, smoothing the tops. Dividing the raspberries and pear pieces evenly, use your fingers to gently poke them into the batter. I like to alternate them, make sure there's a

RECIPE CONTINUES

bit of fruit in every bite, and place some fruit along the edges so it pops out on the sides of the baked cakes.

6. Bake for 15 minutes, then quickly rotate the pans and continue baking until the tops are golden brown, a skewer inserted in the center of each cake comes out clean, and the tops spring back when lightly pressed, 10 to 15 minutes.

7. Let the cakes cool in the pans on wire racks for 30 minutes. Carefully run a small offset spatula between the edges of the pans and the cakes, then flip the pans onto the racks and tap them to make sure the cakes are released. Remove the parchment paper. Use a second rack or a large platter to flip the cakes so they are right-side up on the rack. Let cool completely.

8. FOR THE BROWN BUTTER MAPLE BUTTERCREAM: In a medium saucepan, warm 4 sticks plus 4 tablespoons / 507g of the butter over medium heat, stirring frequently, until completely melted. Once the butter is melted, it will start to foam and bubble. Continue cooking and stirring frequently, for about 12 minutes, or until golden brown and nutty smelling. Remove from the heat, then pour the butter into a heatproof bowl. Let stand at room temperature for 30 minutes. Stir the butter, then cover and refrigerate it, stirring every 20 minutes, for 2 hours.

9. Bring the browned butter back to room temperature.

10. In a stand mixer fitted with the paddle, beat the browned butter and the remaining 3 sticks plus 6 tablespoons / 428g plain butter on medium-high speed, scraping the bowl as needed, until pale and fluffy, about 3 minutes. Scrape the bowl, then beat in the powdered sugar in four batches on low speed, scraping the bowl as needed, just until the powdered sugar is incorporated, about 15 seconds per batch. Once all the powdered sugar is added, beat on medium speed, scraping the bowl as needed, until the buttercream is fluffy and doubles in volume, 2 to 3 minutes. Add the maple syrup, vanilla, salt, and orange zest and beat on low speed for 15 seconds, then increase the speed to high and beat until fully incorporated and the buttercream is pale, airy, and fluffy, about 45 seconds. The buttercream is quite thick.

11. TO ASSEMBLE: Place a cake layer on a large platter or board.

12. Put about 2 cups / 360g of the buttercream into a piping bag fitted with a plain round tip with a ½-inch / 13mm or similar diameter.

13. Holding the pastry tip about 1 inch / 2.5cm above the cake and starting about ¼ inch / 6mm from the edge, pipe a rounded line of buttercream around the perimeter. Pipe a second line inside the first one.

14. Spoon about 1 cup / 300g of the raspberry jam into the center and use a small offset spatula to spread it evenly.

15. Add more buttercream to the piping bag as needed. Pipe zigzags of buttercream in the middle of the cake so it's completely covered. Using a small offset spatula, gently spread the buttercream to fill in any gaps and connect them to the buttercream around the perimeter, while leaving it intact.

16. Carefully place the second cake layer, flat-side up, on top, then gently wiggle it into the buttercream. Add more buttercream to the piping bag as needed.

17. Repeat the above process but pipe a single line of buttercream along the very edge of the cake and skip the jam. Once the top is covered in buttercream, use the tip of a small offset spatula to create some swooshes and texture on top of the cake.

18. Holding the pastry tip about 1 inch / 2.5cm above the cake, pipe 12 large dollops of buttercream on top of the cake. Dip a teaspoon in hot water, then use it to create divots or "bowls" in each dollop of buttercream. Use two small spoons to plop some jam in each buttercream "bowl" (see How to Assemble, Frost, and Cut a Layer Cake, page 53).

19. Arrange a few small flowers and greenery (see Tips for Working with Flowers, page 85) in between the buttercream and jam dollops. Fill in any remaining gaps with a few dehydrated fruit slices and sprinkle the crushed pistachios and freeze-dried raspberries on the buttercream, if desired. The cake (without foliage) keeps covered in the refrigerator for up to 3 days. Remove the cake about 2 hours before serving, so the buttercream has time to soften.

MATCHA WHITE CHOCOLATE MINI CAKES

MAKES EIGHT 3-INCH / 7.5CM TWO-LAYER MINI CAKES

I first discovered matcha when I moved to New York City and worked in the art world. Initially, I ordered matcha lattes just to fit in, even though I thought they tasted like hay. Six years later, I have one every single day. My love for matcha grew even more when I started putting it in my baked goods, and I adore the matcha and white chocolate combo in these two-layer mini cakes. For a more brightly colored green sponge, I recommend using a ceremonial grade matcha versus a culinary grade matcha. It's also important to use high-quality white chocolate and avoid white chocolate chips. Guittard is my favorite brand. French buttercream can be a little scary at first. It gets soupy and can look like it's curdling when you add the butter. Keep beating it, and you'll end up with a silky and not too sweet white chocolate buttercream—it will all be worth it.

MATCHA MINI CAKES

Canola oil spray or canola oil, for the pans
2¼ cups / 315g all-purpose flour
1 tablespoon matcha powder, preferably ceremonial grade
2¼ teaspoons baking powder
¼ teaspoon fine sea salt
2 sticks / 226g unsalted butter, at room temperature and cut into small pieces
2¼ cups / 450g sugar
3 large eggs, at room temperature
1½ teaspoons vanilla extract
1 cup / 240ml whole milk, at room temperature

WHITE CHOCOLATE MATCHA FRENCH BUTTERCREAM

Distilled white vinegar
12¼ ounces / 350g white chocolate, chopped
1 to 2 tablespoons matcha powder, preferably ceremonial grade
1 cup / 200g sugar
4 large eggs
4 large egg yolks
5 sticks / 565g unsalted butter, at cool room temperature and cut into small pieces
1 teaspoon fine sea salt
Whole fresh cherries with stems, for decorating

1. FOR THE MATCHA MINI CAKES: Set a rack in the middle of the oven and preheat to 350°F / 180°C. Spray or brush the sides of eight 3-inch / 7.5cm round mini cake pans with canola oil, then line the bottoms with parchment paper.

2. Sift the flour, matcha powder, and baking powder into a medium bowl. Add the salt.

3. In a stand mixer fitted with the paddle, beat the butter on medium-high speed until pale and smooth, about 3 minutes. Scrape down the bottom and sides of the bowl, then add the sugar and beat until creamy, about 2 minutes. Scrape the bowl, then add the eggs, one at a time, and beat, scraping the bowl before each addition and again at the end, until fully incorporated. Add the vanilla and beat for about 30 seconds to incorporate. Scrape the bowl. On low speed, add the flour mixture in three batches, alternating with the milk in two batches and scraping the bowl before each addition. Mix just until there are no streaks. Do not overmix!

4. Divide the batter evenly among the prepared pans, filling each one just slightly more than halfway. Tap the pans on the counter to even out the batter, then arrange on a baking sheet.

5. Bake until the cakes are lightly golden on top and spring back when lightly pressed, and a skewer inserted in the center of each cake comes out clean, 25 to 30 minutes.

6. Let the cakes cool in the pans on a wire rack for 30 minutes. Jiggle the pans upside down to release the cakes. Remove the parchment paper. Flip the cakes so they are right-side up on the rack. Let cool completely.

7. FOR THE WHITE CHOCOLATE MATCHA FRENCH BUTTERCREAM: Use a paper towel and about ¼ teaspoon of white vinegar to wipe all over the surface of a large heatproof bowl, making sure there aren't any traces of liquid or fat.

RECIPE CONTINUES

8. Fill a medium saucepan with about 1 inch / 2.5cm of water and bring to a simmer over medium-low heat. In the clean heatproof bowl, combine the white chocolate and matcha powder (use more matcha for a deeper green color), then set the bowl over the pan of simmering water, making sure the water does not touch the bottom of the bowl. Warm the white chocolate, stirring occasionally, to incorporate the matcha, until melted and evenly green. Remove the bowl from the pan (careful—it will be warm!) and use a clean kitchen towel to carefully wipe any condensation from the bottom of the bowl. Set aside to cool.

9. In a medium saucepan, combine the sugar and 3 tablespoons water and stir over medium heat until the sugar is completely dissolved. Bring the mixture to a boil, then cook until it becomes a syrup and registers 245°F / 118°C on an instant-read thermometer. As soon as the sugar syrup reaches 245°F / 118°C, remove from the heat.

10. Meanwhile, in a stand mixer fitted with the whisk, whip the whole eggs and egg yolks on medium-high speed until thick and foamy, about 2 minutes. The mixture will be pale yellow and have bubbles.

11. Turn the mixer to medium-low speed. Slowly and carefully pour the hot sugar syrup down the side of the bowl—the bowl will get very hot. Once all the sugar syrup is added, whip on high speed until the bowl returns to room temperature, 6 to 8 minutes. On medium-high speed, gradually start adding half of the butter, one piece at a time, making sure each piece of butter is fully incorporated before adding the next. Switch to the paddle, then continue adding the butter, one piece at a time, and beat until silky and slightly fluffy, 6 to 8 minutes. The buttercream may look soupy or curdled at some point but keep beating and it will come back together. Scrape the bowl, then add the cooled matcha white chocolate mixture and the salt and beat until fully incorporated, about 1 minute. Scrape the bowl and beat for 20 seconds more.

12. TO ASSEMBLE: Once the cakes are completely cool, using a serrated knife, carefully trim the tops. Carefully cut each cake horizontally in half to create two layers. Place the cake bottoms, flat-sides down, on a cake board or serving plate.

13. Put about 2 cups / 410g of buttercream into a piping bag fitted with a plain round tip with a ¼-inch / 6mm or similar diameter.

14. Holding the pastry tip about 1 inch / 2.5cm above a cake bottom and starting from the edge, pipe a rounded ring of buttercream around the perimeter. Pipe a dollop of buttercream in the center, then use a small offset spatula to gently spread the buttercream so it covers the middle of the cake, while leaving the buttercream ring intact. Repeat to top the remaining seven cake bottoms.

15. Carefully place the cake tops, flat-sides up, on top, then gently wiggle them into the buttercream. Add more buttercream to the piping bag as needed. Starting with the pastry tip on the bottom edge of a mini cake and working your way up, pipe dots of buttercream all over the mini cake to cover the entire surface of the cake. Repeat to pipe dots all over the remaining seven mini cakes. Place a cherry in the center on top of each mini cake. The mini cakes keep covered in the refrigerator for up to 2 days. Remove the cakes about 2 hours before serving, so the frosting has time to soften.

BROWN SUGAR PUMPKIN CHESTNUT SALTED CARAMEL SPONGE ROLL

MAKES ONE 13-INCH / 33CM SPONGE ROLL CAKE

This cake is my take on Thanksgiving pie. It's the perfect cozy fall cake and has become a seasonal favorite at the bakery, with many customers ordering it in lieu of the usual holiday desserts.

When making the sponge, be careful not to overmix the batter once you add the flour mixture—this is the key to keeping the cake light and airy. Both the chestnut cream and the salted caramel will keep in the fridge for up to 3 weeks, so they're perfect for prepping in advance. And if you're short on time, store-bought chestnut cream (like Crème de Marrons de l'Ardèche) is a great shortcut.

BROWN SUGAR SPONGE ROLL

Canola oil spray or canola oil, for the pan
Powdered sugar, for dusting
1 cup / 140g all-purpose flour
1¼ teaspoons baking powder
6 large eggs, at room temperature
½ teaspoon fine sea salt
1 cup plus 2 tablespoons / 225g granulated sugar
½ cup plus 2 tablespoons / 125g (packed) light brown sugar
4 tablespoons / 55g unsalted butter

PUMPKIN WHIPPED CREAM

2 cups plus 2 tablespoons / 510ml heavy cream
2 tablespoons vanilla bean paste
¼ teaspoon fine sea salt
6 tablespoons / 45g powdered sugar, plus more for dusting
1 teaspoon ground cinnamon
1 cup plus 2 tablespoons / 255g canned pure pumpkin puree (not pumpkin pie mix)

ASSEMBLY

About ⅓ cup / 80ml Salted Caramel (recipe follows)
About ⅓ cup / 100g chestnut cream, homemade (recipe follows) or store-bought

1. FOR THE BROWN SUGAR SPONGE ROLL: Set a rack in the middle of the oven and preheat to 375°F / 190°C. Spray or brush the bottom and sides of one 13 × 18-inch / 33 × 45cm or similarly sized baking sheet with canola oil and line the bottom with parchment paper. Dust a similarly sized clean tea towel with powdered sugar and set it near the oven.

2. Sift the flour and baking powder into a small bowl.

3. In a stand mixer fitted with the paddle, beat the eggs and salt on high speed until fully combined, about 1 minute. Scrape down the bottom and sides of the bowl, then add the granulated sugar and brown sugar and beat until pale, thick, and creamy, about 5 minutes.

4. Remove the bowl from the stand mixer. Scrape the bowl, then gently fold in the flour mixture in three batches with a rubber spatula just until there are no streaks. Do not overmix!

5. In a small saucepan, bring the butter to a boil over medium heat. Carefully pour the hot butter into the batter and gently fold just until it's incorporated.

6. Gently spread the batter evenly in the prepared pan, smoothing the top. Bake until the cake is golden brown on top and feels spongy when lightly pressed, about 10 minutes.

7. Let the cake cool slightly in the pan on a wire rack, then carefully flip it out onto the powdered sugar–dusted tea towel. Remove the parchment paper.

8. Starting on one of the short sides, quickly but gently roll the cake up into a tight spiral. Arrange the roll so the seam is on the bottom and let cool for about 30 minutes while you prepare the whipped cream.

9. FOR THE PUMPKIN WHIPPED CREAM: In a stand mixer fitted with the whisk, combine the heavy cream, vanilla bean paste, and salt. Sift in the powdered sugar

RECIPE CONTINUES

and cinnamon, then whip on medium-high speed for 3 minutes, scraping the bowl as needed. Increase the speed to high and whip until stiff peaks form, 2 to 3 minutes more.

10. Remove the bowl from the stand mixer. Scrape the bowl, then gently fold in the pumpkin puree with a rubber spatula until just combined. It should be light orange in color.

11. TO ASSEMBLE: Gently unroll the cake. It will have deflated a bit. Using a small offset spatula, spread an even layer of the salted caramel across the entire surface of the cake. Repeat with the chestnut cream. Carefully spread the pumpkin whipped cream across the entire surface of the cake, completely covering the chestnut cream. Carefully roll the cake back into a spiral, making sure the seam is on the bottom.

12. Dust with powdered sugar and serve right away. The cake is best the day it's assembled, but it keeps covered in the refrigerator for up to 1 day.

Salted Caramel

MAKES ABOUT 1 CUP / 240ML

½ cup / 100g sugar
3 tablespoons salted butter, cut into small pieces
¾ cup plus 2 tablespoons / 210ml heavy cream
⅛ teaspoon Maldon sea salt

1. Add the sugar to a heavy-bottomed medium saucepan that's wide enough for the sugar to be in a thin, even layer. Set the pan over medium heat and cook the sugar, without stirring, until it melts and caramelizes—it's fine to gently swirl the pan a few times to even out the caramelization. It should be light golden brown and not dark, or the caramel will be too bitter. While whisking, gradually add the salted butter. Slowly pour in the heavy cream, whisking vigorously to prevent lumps, until the mixture is smooth. Continue cooking the caramel, without whisking or stirring—it may bubble up—until slightly thickened, about 5 minutes. Remove from the heat, then add the Maldon salt and whisk briefly just to incorporate it.

2. Pour the caramel into an 8 ounce / 240ml jar and let cool, uncovered, to room temperature.

3. The caramel will still be very fluid, but if cooked properly, it will continue to thicken as it cools. The caramel keeps in an airtight container in the refrigerator for up to 3 weeks.

Chestnut Cream

MAKES ABOUT 2 CUPS / 600G

1 cup / 200g sugar
½ teaspoon vanilla bean paste
1 (15.5-ounce / 439g) can chestnut puree

1. In a medium saucepan, combine the sugar and 1 cup / 240ml water and bring to a simmer over medium-high heat, stirring occasionally. By the time it comes to a boil, the sugar should be dissolved, and the liquid should be clear. Remove from the heat, then stir in the vanilla bean paste. Pour the mixture into a small bowl and let cool to room temperature. Do not clean the saucepan.

2. Add the chestnut puree to the same saucepan and set it over medium-low heat. While stirring, slowly pour in the cooled sugar syrup. Cook the mixture, stirring occasionally, until the chestnut cream is thick and dark, 25 to 30 minutes.

3. Remove from the heat and let cool to room temperature. The cream will continue to thicken as it cools. The chestnut cream keeps in an airtight container in the refrigerator for up to 3 weeks.

DOUX

LEMON OLIVE OIL LAVENDER CAKE

MAKES ONE 8-INCH / 20CM CAKE

Light, spongy, tangy, and not overly sweet, this cake is an ode to my two uncles. My uncle Jean-Jacques lives in Menton, a town in southwest France that's not far from Provence's iconic lavender fields and hosts a citrus festival every February. Jean-Jacques has the most beautiful lemon trees in his garden and makes his own limoncello and lemon marmalade. My uncle Mike has an olive farm in Kaukapakapa, New Zealand, and makes some of the best olive oil I've ever had—no bias at all here. Different from typical Italian olive oil, his has a grassiness I love. This cake contains a lot of olive oil, and the flavor really comes through, so be sure to use a high-quality oil. I promise it's worth it.

LEMON OLIVE OIL CAKE

- Canola oil spray or canola oil, for the pan
- 1¾ cups plus 3 tablespoons / 270g all-purpose flour
- 1 teaspoon baking powder
- 1 teaspoon baking soda
- ½ teaspoon fine sea salt
- 1⅓ cups / 265g sugar
- 5 teaspoons grated lemon zest (from 2 medium lemons)
- ¾ cup plus 2 tablespoons / 210ml olive oil
- 3 large eggs, at room temperature
- ¾ cup / 180ml buttermilk, at room temperature

LAVENDER SWISS MERINGUE BUTTERCREAM

- Distilled white vinegar
- 105g egg whites (about 3 large), at room temperature
- 1 cup / 200g sugar
- 2 sticks plus 2 tablespoons / 256g unsalted butter, at cool room temperature and cut into small pieces
- 5 tablespoons plus 2 teaspoons / 85g Lavender-Infused Butter (recipe follows), at cool room temperature and cut into small pieces
- ¼ teaspoon fine sea salt

ASSEMBLY

- About ¾ cup / 185g Lemon Curd (recipe follows)
- Small edible flowers (see page 88), for decorating

1. **FOR THE LEMON OLIVE OIL CAKE:** Set a rack in the middle of the oven and preheat to 350°F / 180°C. Spray or brush the sides of one 8-inch / 20cm round cake pan with canola oil, then line the bottom with parchment paper.

2. Sift the flour, baking powder, and baking soda into a medium bowl. Add the salt.

3. In a stand mixer, combine the sugar and lemon zest and use your fingers to massage the mixture, releasing the citrus oils. Add the olive oil, then use the paddle attachment to beat on medium speed until fully incorporated and the mixture looks like wet sand, about 30 seconds. Add the eggs, one at a time, and beat on medium-low speed, scraping down the bottom and sides of the bowl before each addition and again at the end, until the mixture is thick and creamy. Add the flour mixture in three batches, alternating with the buttermilk in two batches and scraping the bowl before each addition. Mix just until there are no streaks. Once all the flour is added, beat on medium speed for 30 seconds to make sure it is fully incorporated.

4. Pour the batter into the prepared pan, smoothing the top. Bake for 20 minutes, then quickly rotate the pan and continue baking until the top springs back when lightly pressed and a skewer inserted in the center of the cake comes out clean, 15 to 20 minutes.

5. Let the cake cool in the pan on a wire rack for 30 minutes. Carefully run a small offset spatula between the edges of the pan and the cake, then flip the pan onto the rack and tap it to make sure the cake is released. Remove the parchment paper. Use a second rack or a plate to flip the cake so it's right-side up on the rack. Let cool completely.

6. **FOR THE LAVENDER SWISS MERINGUE BUTTERCREAM:** (Before starting, read How to Make Swiss Meringue

RECIPE CONTINUES

Buttercream, page 129.) Fill a medium saucepan with about 1 inch / 2.5cm of water and bring to a simmer over medium-low heat.

7. Use a paper towel and about ¼ teaspoon of white vinegar to wipe all over the surface of a large heatproof bowl and the bowl of a stand mixer, making sure there aren't any traces of liquid or fat.

8. In the clean heatproof bowl, combine the egg whites and sugar, then set the bowl over the pan of simmering water, making sure the water does not touch the bottom of the bowl. Heat the mixture, whisking constantly, until it registers 130°F / 54°C on an instant-read thermometer, 3 to 4 minutes.

9. Transfer the mixture to the clean bowl of the stand mixer. Using the whisk attachment, whip on high speed until stiff peaks form, 8 to 10 minutes. Switch to the paddle attachment. Gradually start adding the plain butter and the lavender-infused butter in small batches and beat on medium-high speed, scraping the bowl as needed, until all the butter has been added. Beat on high speed until the buttercream is fluffy and has air bubbles, about 1 minute. Add the salt and beat on low speed until fully combined, about 30 seconds.

10. TO ASSEMBLE: Place the cake, flat-side down, on a cake plate or stand.

11. Using a rubber spatula, put a large dollop of the buttercream on top of the cake. Use a small offset spatula to spread the buttercream on top of the cake, then use the tip of the spatula to create some swooshes and texture on top.

12. Scoop about ½ cup / 125g of the lemon curd on top of the buttercream in the center of the cake. Using a small offset spatula, spread the curd in an even layer, leaving ½ inch / 13mm of exposed buttercream around the edges.

13. Use a small spoon to dollop about 1 teaspoon of lemon curd at a point on the edge of the buttercream. Gently spread the dollop to the edge of the cake and allow it to drip halfway down the side. Repeat this step five to seven times depending on how many drips you would like.

14. Gently press the flowers or petals into the curd (see Tips for Working with Flowers, page 85). The cake (without flowers) keeps covered in the refrigerator for up to 2 days. Remove the cake about 2 hours before serving, so the buttercream has time to soften.

Lavender-Infused Butter

MAKES ⅔ CUP / 150G

1 stick plus 4 tablespoons / 168g unsalted butter, cut into small pieces
2 tablespoons culinary lavender

1. In a small saucepan, melt the butter over medium-low heat. Remove from the heat, then stir in the lavender, cover, and let stand for 30 minutes.

2. Pour through a fine-mesh sieve set over a medium bowl, pressing on the lavender to extract as much flavor as possible (discard the lavender). Cover and refrigerate, stirring every 20 minutes, until the butter starts to firm up, about 1 hour, then leave it alone to chill completely, at least 1 hour and up to 1 week. The butter can also be well wrapped and frozen for up to 2 months; thaw in the refrigerator overnight.

Lemon Curd

MAKES 2 CUPS / 500G

120g egg yolks (about 8 large), at room temperature
½ cup plus 1 tablespoon / 115g sugar
½ cup / 120ml freshly squeezed lemon juice (from 3 medium lemons)
1 stick plus 5 tablespoons / 183g unsalted butter, at room temperature
⅛ teaspoon fine sea salt

1. Fill a medium saucepan with about 1 inch / 2.5cm of water and bring to a simmer over medium-low heat. In a large heatproof bowl, combine the egg yolks, sugar, and lemon juice, then set the bowl over the pan of simmering water, making sure the water does not touch the bottom of the bowl. Cook the mixture, stirring constantly, until it registers 170° to 180°F / 77° to 82°C on an instant-read thermometer.

2. Pour through a fine-mesh sieve set over a large bowl. While the mixture is still hot, gradually but quickly whisk in the butter, one piece at a time, making sure the butter gets completely incorporated before adding the next piece. Whisk in the salt. If you want to seal the curd in jars for longer term storage, do so while it's still hot (see How to Can Jams and Curds, page 187).

3. Otherwise, press plastic wrap directly onto the surface to prevent a skin from forming and let cool for about 15 minutes, then refrigerate until cold. The curd keeps in an airtight container in the refrigerator for up to 7 days.

VOLLRATH

How to
MAKE SWISS MERINGUE BUTTERCREAM

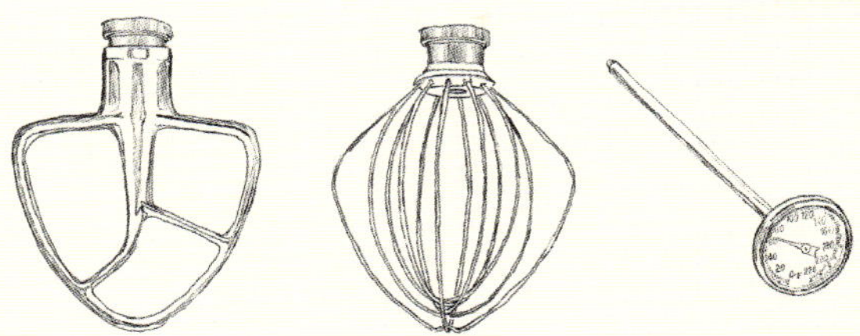

Swiss meringue buttercream is my favorite because it isn't overly sweet, which makes it ideal if you're working with subtle flavors like herbs and florals. Many buttercreams are made with a lot of powdered sugar, leaving you with an overly sugary aftertaste. Swiss meringue buttercream is made by heating egg whites and granulated sugar, then adding butter and beating it all until wonderfully light and fluffy. It's very easy to pipe, whether you're assembling a layer cake or adding decorations.

Making Swiss meringue buttercream can be slightly intimidating at first, but I promise that once you go through the process a few times, you'll be able to do it with your eyes closed. For a successful buttercream, which is nice and fluffy, airy, and silky, there are a few rules to follow. Throughout the book, you'll find recipes for a variety of Swiss meringue buttercreams, including several made with infused butters (see How to Infuse Butter, page 39), but they all follow the same basic principles.

EIGHT RULES FOR MAKING SWISS MERINGUE BUTTERCREAM

1. Before you start, use a paper towel and white vinegar to thoroughly wipe the inside of a large heatproof bowl and a stand mixer bowl, making sure there aren't any traces of liquid or fat. There cannot be a single drop of liquid or fat in either bowl or the egg whites will not form a meringue.

2. It's easier to separate eggs when they're cold, so start with straight-from-the-fridge eggs. Using the eggshell to separate the whites from the yolk can break the yolk more easily, so I prefer to use my hands. I crack an egg and wiggle it in my hand so the white falls into a small bowl below. Then, to make sure no yolk gets into the white, I transfer that white to another bowl and use the original bowl to catch the white of the next egg.

3. The temperature of the butter is very important, as you need it soft enough that it's absorbed into the meringue but not so soft that it melts from the warmth. Aim for cool room temperature, which should feel slightly cool to the touch and should indent slightly, not sink, when you press your finger into it.

4. To make a Swiss meringue, you need to cook egg whites and granulated sugar to 130°F / 54°C and the best way to do this is over a water bath. Start by filling a medium saucepan with about 1 inch / 2.5cm of water and bring the water to a simmer. Next, put the egg whites and sugar in the large heatproof bowl you cleaned with white vinegar and set it over the pan. Make sure the bowl doesn't touch the simmering water.

5. When cooking the egg white and sugar mixture, you can use an instant-read thermometer to test when it is ready, but it's even better if you can learn to identify how it should look and feel. It should be almost translucent and smooth and sticky to the touch. If you rub the mixture between your fingers, you shouldn't feel any grains of sugar. Once the mixture is ready, remove it from the bowl and use a clean kitchen towel to wipe the bottom, so no condensation can drip into your meringue.

6. Once you transfer the egg white and sugar mixture to the stand mixer, it's really important to whip it to stiff peaks, which should be done on high speed and typically takes 8 to 10 minutes. If you're unsure, remove the whisk attachment from the stand mixer and hold it upside down. If the peaks remain very straight, the meringue has the right consistency.

7. Incorporating butter into your Swiss meringue requires patience. With the paddle attached and the mixer on medium-high speed, gradually add the butter, piece by piece, letting each piece incorporate into the meringue before adding more and scraping the bottom and sides of the bowl as needed.

8. Once all the butter is added, beat the buttercream on high speed for about 1 minute. At this point, the buttercream will go through several stages, looking too soft at first, then slightly curdled, but don't panic. Just keep beating and you'll soon see the mixture come back together with a cloud-like texture. Once it's airy and fluffy, stop! This is how I like it. However, if you're planning to completely cover a cake and want a really smooth, sleek surface, beat the buttercream a bit longer so it has a tighter consistency.

MAKING SWISS MERINGUE BUTTERCREAM IN ADVANCE

Most of the time, you'll make buttercream the day you plan to serve your cake, but it can actually be made ahead and stored in an airtight container in the refrigerator for up to 7 days. This is also great if you happen to have leftover buttercream and want to save it for another cake.

TWO WAYS TO FIX SWISS MERINGUE BUTTERCREAM

Swiss meringue buttercream can be a little temperamental, especially depending on the weather. If it's cold outside, it's more likely your buttercream will curdle, because the butter is too cold, and if it's too hot, the butter could be too soft, making for soupy buttercream. Thankfully, there's always a solution.

Once all the butter has been added, and you're beating the buttercream, it may look curdled or separated, but if it continues to appear curdled after that minute, the butter was too cold. Take a small portion of the buttercream (about one-eighth of the total amount) and gently melt it in the microwave (don't let it come to a boil). Slowly incorporate the melted buttercream back into the rest, beating on medium-high speed, to warm up the buttercream and bring it together.

On the other hand, if you've beaten your buttercream for about 1 minute and it appears too soupy, the butter was too soft. Your best bet is to place the stand mixer bowl in the refrigerator to chill the buttercream for 15 to 30 minutes, then beat it on medium-high speed for about 30 seconds until light and fluffy.

Vanilla Bean Swiss Meringue Buttercream

MAKES ABOUT 3½ CUPS / 575G BUTTERCREAM
(ENOUGH FOR ONE FULLY EXPOSED 8-INCH / 20CM TWO-LAYER CAKE)

This classic buttercream can be paired with almost any cake. It's simpler than my other buttercreams, so if you want to make a cake with a bit less fuss, use it in place of my basil Swiss meringue buttercream (page 93), blood orange Swiss meringue buttercream (page 141), prosecco Swiss meringue buttercream (page 146), or lavender Swiss meringue buttercream (page 124).

Distilled white vinegar
140g egg whites (about 4 large), at room temperature
1 cup / 200g sugar
3 sticks / 339g unsalted butter, at cool room temperature and cut into small pieces
1 teaspoon vanilla bean paste
⅛ teaspoon fine sea salt

1. Fill a medium saucepan with about 1 inch / 2.5cm of water and bring to a simmer over medium-low heat.

2. Use a paper towel and about ¼ teaspoon of white vinegar to wipe all over the surface of a large heatproof bowl and the bowl of a stand mixer, making sure there aren't any traces of liquid or fat.

3. In the clean heatproof bowl, combine the egg whites and sugar, then set the bowl over the pan of simmering water, making sure the water does not touch the bottom of the bowl. Heat the mixture, whisking constantly, until it registers 130°F / 54°C on an instant-read thermometer, 3 to 4 minutes.

4. Transfer the mixture to the clean bowl of the stand mixer. Using the whisk attachment, whip on high speed until stiff peaks form, 8 to 10 minutes. Switch to the paddle attachment. Gradually start adding the butter in small batches and beat on medium-high speed, scraping the bottom and sides of the bowl as needed, until all the butter has been added. Beat on high speed until the buttercream is fluffy and has air bubbles, about 1 minute. Add the vanilla bean paste and salt and beat on low speed until fully combined, about 30 seconds.

COFFEE WALNUT MERINGUE CAKE

MAKES ONE 9-INCH / 23CM CAKE

This cake is a nod to the classic gâteau aux noix from my beloved Périgord region. Inspired by a base recipe from my mother, I wanted to give this cake a fresh spin. While the traditional version is often quite dense, I've taken mine in a more airy and spongy direction and incorporated crunchy walnuts and soft coffee notes for added flavor. Instead of topping it with a traditional buttercream, I've opted for a light coffee-infused meringue that has dramatic visual appeal and a unique texture that's crisp on the outside yet soft and almost melty on the inside.

COFFEE WALNUT CAKE

Canola oil spray or canola oil, for the pan
1¼ cups / 175g all-purpose flour
2¼ teaspoons baking powder
¼ teaspoon fine sea salt
1 stick plus 5 tablespoons / 183g unsalted butter, at room temperature
¾ cup plus 2 tablespoons / 175g sugar
3 large eggs, at room temperature
2 tablespoons brewed espresso, cooled
1 cup / 120g walnut halves, roughly chopped

MERINGUE

Distilled white vinegar
140g egg whites (about 4 large), at room temperature
¾ cup plus 2 tablespoons / 175g sugar
1 tablespoon cornstarch
¾ teaspoon apple cider vinegar
¾ teaspoon coffee extract

1. FOR THE COFFEE WALNUT CAKE: Set a rack in the middle of the oven and preheat to 350°F / 180°C. Spray or brush the sides of a 9-inch / 23cm springform pan with canola oil, then line the bottom with parchment paper.

2. Sift the flour and baking powder into a small bowl. Add the salt.

3. In a stand mixer fitted with the paddle, beat the butter on medium-high speed until pale and creamy, about 2 minutes. Scrape down the bottom and sides of the bowl, then add the sugar and beat on medium-high speed until fully incorporated and fluffy, about 2 minutes. Scrape the bowl again, then add the eggs, one at a time, and beat on medium speed, scraping the bowl before each addition and again at the end, until fully incorporated. On low speed, add the flour mixture in three batches, alternating with the cooled espresso in two batches and scraping the bowl before each addition. Mix just until there are no streaks. Do not overmix!

4. Remove the bowl from the stand mixer, then gently fold in the walnuts with a rubber spatula until incorporated. Pour the batter into the prepared pan and set aside.

5. FOR THE MERINGUE: Use a paper towel and about ¼ teaspoon of white vinegar to wipe all over the surface of the bowl of a stand mixer, making sure there aren't any traces of liquid or fat.

6. Add the egg whites to the clean bowl of the stand mixer and use the whisk attachment to whip on medium-high speed until stiff peaks form, 3 to 4 minutes. Gradually add the sugar, 1 tablespoon at a time, and continue whipping until very stiff peaks form, 4 to 5 minutes.

7. Remove the bowl from the stand mixer, then add the cornstarch, vinegar, and coffee extract and gently fold with a rubber spatula until incorporated, being careful not to deflate the meringue.

8. Spoon the meringue over the cake batter, using a small offset spatula to create swoops and peaks for a dramatic texture. Bake until a long skewer inserted between the cracks in the meringue comes out with soft cake crumbs, about 1 hour. The meringue should rise and turn golden brown and will be crunchy on the outside and soft like a marshmallow on the inside.

9. Let the cake cool completely in the pan on a wire rack.

10. Once the cake is cool, run a small offset spatula around the edges of the pan to loosen the meringue. Place the pan on a tall, narrow object, such as a sturdy glass or can, and carefully release the springform ring, letting it fall away.

11. Use a large serving spatula to carefully remove the cake from the base of the springform pan and place onto a serving plate. The cake is best the day it's made, but it keeps covered in the refrigerator for 1 or 2 days.

CHOCOLATE MOUSSE CAKE

MAKES ONE 8-INCH / 20CM CAKE

This is my "no fuss" version of Alain Ducasse's iconic Louis XV, a multilayered chocolate and hazelnut dessert. Mine may not have quite the precision of the original and is more rustic, but I promise that it's just as delicious. With layers of chocolate sponge, chocolate craquant, and chocolate mousse, all wrapped in a ganache-like chocolate glaze, then topped with raspberries and drizzled with honey, it's very much a project cake. But if you are a chocolate lover, this one's for you. For the best results—and to keep this project manageable—I recommend making the sponge, craquant, and mousse the day before, so the mousse has time to set, and then making the glaze the day you plan to serve the cake.

CHOCOLATE CAKE

Canola oil spray or canola oil, for the pan
½ teaspoon instant coffee
½ cup / 120ml boiling water
¾ cup plus 2 tablespoons / 125g all-purpose flour
3 tablespoons unsweetened Dutch-process cocoa powder
¾ teaspoon baking soda
½ teaspoon baking powder
¼ teaspoon fine sea salt
6 tablespoons / 90ml buttermilk, at room temperature
3 tablespoons sour cream, at room temperature
¾ cup plus 2 tablespoons / 175g sugar
⅓ cup / 80ml canola oil
1 large egg, at room temperature
¾ teaspoon vanilla extract

CHOCOLATE CRAQUANT

4 ounces / 115g dark chocolate, preferably 72% cacao, chopped
4 ounces / 115g milk chocolate, chopped
1 cup / 35g cornflakes
¼ teaspoon fine sea salt

CHOCOLATE MOUSSE

5 ounces / 140g dark chocolate, preferably 72% cacao, chopped
⅛ teaspoon Maldon sea salt
1¾ cups / 420ml heavy cream
1¼ teaspoons vanilla extract

CHOCOLATE GLAZE

15 ounces / 425g dark chocolate, preferably 64% cacao, chopped
2 cups / 480ml heavy cream
2 teaspoons light corn syrup
¾ teaspoon Maldon sea salt

ASSEMBLY

About 2 cups / 240g fresh raspberries
2 tablespoons honey

1. FOR THE CHOCOLATE CAKE: Set a rack in the middle of the oven and preheat to 350°F / 180°C. Spray or brush the sides of one 8-inch / 20cm round cake pan with canola oil, then line the bottom with parchment paper.

2. In a small bowl, combine the instant coffee and boiling water and stir to dissolve. Put the mixture in the refrigerator to cool.

3. Sift the flour, cocoa powder, baking soda, and baking powder into a medium bowl. Add the fine salt.

4. In a small bowl, combine the buttermilk and sour cream and whisk to fully combine.

5. In a stand mixer fitted with the paddle, beat the sugar and canola oil on medium speed until they're combined and the mixture looks like wet sand, about 30 seconds. Scrape down the bottom and sides of the bowl, then add the egg and beat until fully incorporated. Scrape the bowl, then add the vanilla, beat for 30 seconds to incorporate, and scrape again. On low speed, add the flour mixture in three batches, alternating with the buttermilk mixture in two batches and scraping the bowl before each addition. Mix just until there are no streaks. On low speed, gradually add the cooled coffee. Mix for 30 seconds, then scrape the bowl one final time. Do not overmix! The batter will be very dark in color and very loose.

6. Pour the batter into the prepared pan, smoothing the top. Bake until the cake springs back when lightly pressed and a skewer inserted in the center of the cake comes out clean, about 30 minutes.

RECIPE CONTINUES

7. Let the cake cool in the pan on a wire rack for 30 minutes. Carefully run a small offset spatula between the edges of the pan and the cake, then flip the pan onto the rack and tap it to make sure the cake is released. Remove the parchment paper. Use a second rack or a plate to flip the cake so it's right-side up on the rack. Let cool completely.

8. FOR THE CHOCOLATE CRAQUANT: Line one 8-inch / 20cm round cake pan with parchment paper. Place the cooled chocolate sponge cake, flat-side up, inside.

9. Fill a medium saucepan with about 1 inch / 2.5cm of water and bring to a simmer over medium-low heat. In a large heatproof bowl, combine the dark and milk chocolates, then set the bowl over the pan of simmering water, making sure the water does not touch the bottom of the bowl. Warm the chocolate, stirring occasionally, until melted. Remove the bowl from the pan (careful—it will be warm!) and use a clean kitchen towel to carefully wipe any condensation from the bottom of the bowl. Add the cornflakes and fine salt and stir to break the cereal into small pieces and completely cover in chocolate.

10. Spread a thin, even layer of the warm chocolate craquant on top of the cake, making sure to completely cover the cake and trying to make it as flat as possible—this is important because it will be the base of the cake. Cover the pan with plastic wrap and refrigerate for 2 to 3 hours, or until the craquant is set. If you're in a hurry, you can freeze it for 30 minutes.

11. Once the craquant is set, line an 8-inch / 20cm adjustable cake ring with acetate or parchment paper cut to fit inside the ring. Set the lined cake ring on a slightly larger plate.

12. Run a small offset spatula between the edges of the pan and the cake, then flip the cake onto a plate so the craquant layer is on the bottom. Remove the parchment paper, then carefully place the cake, craquant-layer down, inside the prepared cake ring. Adjust the cake ring as needed so it's flush with the cake. Keep refrigerated while you make the mousse.

13. FOR THE CHOCOLATE MOUSSE: Fill a medium saucepan with about 1 inch / 2.5cm of water and bring to a simmer over medium-low heat. In a large heatproof bowl, combine the chocolate and Maldon salt, then set the bowl over the pan of simmering water, making sure the water does not touch the bottom of the bowl. Warm the chocolate, stirring occasionally, until melted. Remove the bowl from the pan (careful—it will be warm!) and use a clean kitchen towel to carefully wipe any condensation from the bottom of the bowl. Keep warm.

14. In a small saucepan, warm ½ cup / 120ml of the heavy cream over low heat just until steam starts to rise from the surface; do not let it come to a simmer or bubble. Immediately pour it over the melted chocolate and salt. Using a rubber spatula, start gently stirring in the middle of the bowl and working your way outward to emulsify the mixture. Let cool slightly.

15. In a stand mixer fitted with the whisk, combine the remaining 1¼ cups / 300ml heavy cream and the vanilla and whip on medium-high speed until stiff peaks form, about 6 minutes. Add about ½ cup / 50g of the whipped cream to the slightly cooled chocolate mixture and gently fold them together with a rubber spatula. Add the remaining whipped cream and gently fold until just combined—you want to keep the fluffy, airy texture.

16. Fill a piping bag with the chocolate mousse and use scissors to cut the tip of the bag so it has a 1-inch / 2.5cm opening. Starting on the outside edge of the cake, pipe a spiral of mousse all the way to the center of the cake with no gaps. Repeat to create a second layer, then use a small offset spatula to smooth and spread the mousse all the way to the edge of the cake ring, creating a thick, even layer of mousse.

17. Loosely cover the cake and refrigerate overnight to set the mousse. If you're in a hurry, you can freeze it for 1 hour.

18. Once the chocolate mousse has set, run a small offset spatula between the edges of the cake and the cake ring, then gently remove the ring. You should now see three distinct layers: the craquant, the sponge, and the mousse.

19. **FOR THE CHOCOLATE GLAZE:** Add the chocolate to a large heatproof bowl.

20. In a small saucepan, warm the heavy cream over medium heat just until steam starts to rise from the surface; do not let it come to a simmer or bubble. Immediately pour the hot cream over the chocolate and stir with a rubber spatula until the chocolate is melted and fully combined with the cream. Add the corn syrup and Maldon salt and stir to incorporate. Let the glaze stand at room temperature until completely cool. Once cool, the glaze should be thick, glossy, and just slightly runny. If the glaze is still very runny, let it stand at room temperature to firm up for about 10 minutes before using.

21. **TO ASSEMBLE:** Place the cake, craquant-layer down, on an 8-inch / 20cm cardboard cake round, then set the cake round on a wire rack set over a baking sheet.

22. Pour the glaze over the mousse to cover the top and sides of the cake. Use the tip of a small offset spatula to create some swooshes and texture on the top and sides of the cake.

23. Top the cake with the raspberries, then use a pastry brush to gently dab the berries with honey so they shine—if it's winter, you may need to briefly warm the honey before using it. The cake keeps covered in the refrigerator for up to 3 days. Remove the cake about 1 hour before serving, so it can warm to room temperature.

BROWN BUTTER BAY LEAF MASCARPONE TAHINI CAKE

MAKES ONE 6-INCH / 15CM AND 8-INCH / 20CM TWO-LAYER CAKE

While it's simple and quick to prepare, this cake offers an elevated take on the classic yogurt cake. In lieu of yogurt, the mascarpone imparts a rich, velvety texture and deeper flavor, while the bay leaf–infused browned butter adds an additional layer of complexity. The whipped cream, enhanced with orange zest and tahini, complements the cake perfectly.

BROWN BUTTER BAY LEAF MASCARPONE CAKE

1 stick plus 6 tablespoons / 198g unsalted butter, cut into small pieces
4 dried bay leaves, roughly chopped
Canola oil spray or canola oil, for the pans
2 cups / 280g all-purpose flour
2 teaspoons baking powder
1¼ cups / 250g granulated sugar
1 teaspoon fine sea salt
¾ cup / 170g mascarpone, at room temperature
4 large eggs, at room temperature
¾ teaspoon vanilla extract

TAHINI ORANGE WHIPPED CREAM

2 cups / 480ml heavy cream, cold
5 teaspoons powdered sugar, sifted
1 tablespoon well-mixed tahini
¼ teaspoon grated orange zest (from 1 medium orange)

ASSEMBLY

1 large flower (see page 88), for decorating

1. FOR THE BROWN BUTTER BAY LEAF MASCARPONE CAKE: In a small saucepan, warm the butter over medium-low heat, stirring frequently, until completely melted. Once the butter is melted, it will start to foam and bubble. Continue cooking and stirring frequently, for about 8 minutes, or until golden brown and nutty smelling. Remove from the heat, then pour the butter into a heatproof bowl. Stir in the bay leaves, cover, and let stand for 30 minutes.

2. Pour through a fine-mesh sieve set over a small bowl, pressing on the bay leaves to extract as much flavor as possible (discard the bay leaves). Let the butter cool completely.

3. Set a rack in the middle of the oven and preheat to 350°F / 180°C. Spray or brush the sides of one 6-inch / 15cm round cake pan and one 8-inch / 20cm round cake pan with canola oil, then line the bottoms with parchment paper.

4. Sift the flour and baking powder into a large bowl. Add the granulated sugar and salt and whisk to combine.

5. In a stand mixer fitted with the paddle, beat the mascarpone on medium-high speed until lighter and creamier, about 30 seconds. Scrape down the bottom and sides of the bowl, then add the eggs, one at a time, and beat on medium speed, scraping the bowl before each addition and again at the end, until fully incorporated. Add the vanilla and beat for 30 seconds to incorporate. Add the cooled bay leaf–infused brown butter and beat on medium-low speed until incorporated, about 30 seconds, then scrape the bowl. Add the flour and sugar mixture in three batches and mix on low speed, scraping the bowl before each addition, just until there are no streaks. Do not overmix!

6. Pour about two-thirds of the batter into the prepared 8-inch / 20cm cake pan, smoothing the top. Pour the remaining batter into the prepared 6-inch / 15cm cake pan, smoothing the top. Bake for 15 minutes, then quickly rotate the pans and continue baking until the cakes are slightly golden on top and a skewer inserted in the centers comes out clean, about 15 minutes more for the 6-inch / 15cm cake and 20 minutes more for the 8-inch / 20cm cake.

RECIPE CONTINUES

7. Let the cakes cool in the pans on a wire rack for 30 minutes. Carefully run a small offset spatula between the edges of the pans and the cakes, then flip the pans onto the rack and tap them to make sure the cakes are released. Remove the parchment paper. Use a second rack or a plate to flip the cakes so they are right-side up on the rack. Let cool completely.

8. FOR THE TAHINI ORANGE WHIPPED CREAM: In a stand mixer fitted with the whisk, combine the heavy cream, powdered sugar, and tahini and whip on medium-high speed for 3 minutes. Increase the speed to high and whip until stiff peaks form, 2 to 3 minutes. Add the orange zest and whip for a few seconds just until incorporated.

9. TO ASSEMBLE: Place the 8-inch / 20cm cake, flat-side down, on a cake plate or stand. Using a rubber spatula, spread about two-thirds of the tahini orange whipped cream on top of the cake. Use the tip of a small offset spatula to create some swooshes and texture on the top of the cake. Gently place the 6-inch / 15cm cake on top, making sure it's in the center. Using a small offset spatula, spread the remaining whipped cream on top of the cake. Use the tip of the spatula to create some swooshes and texture on the top of the cake.

10. Arrange the large flower on top of the cake (see Tips for Working with Flowers, page 85). The cake is best the day it's assembled.

BLOOD ORANGE OLIVE OIL PRINCESS CAKE

MAKES ONE 8-INCH / 20CM CAKE

I've always loved the look of a princess cake, but I don't like fondant or artificial food coloring. As I thought about how to mimic the cake's smooth, colorful dome using more natural ingredients, blood orange came to mind. With its deep pink tones, this citrus fruit can be combined with powdered sugar to create a thin and slightly glossy baby pink glaze, but it can also be used to make a vibrant pink curd to layer inside the cake. When making the glaze, you can play around with the thickness and color, keeping in mind that the blood orange juice will be the deepest pink at the height of the season in January and February.

BLOOD ORANGE OLIVE OIL CAKE

Canola oil spray or canola oil, for the pan
1½ cups / 210g all-purpose flour
1 teaspoon baking powder
½ teaspoon baking soda
¼ teaspoon fine sea salt
1 cup plus 2 tablespoons / 225g granulated sugar
1 tablespoon grated blood orange zest (from 1 blood orange)
2 tablespoons freshly squeezed blood orange juice (from 1 blood orange), at room temperature
½ cup / 120ml buttermilk, at room temperature
½ cup plus 2 tablespoons / 150ml extra-virgin olive oil
2 large eggs, at room temperature

BLOOD ORANGE SWISS MERINGUE BUTTERCREAM

Distilled white vinegar
105g egg whites (about 3 large), at room temperature
1 cup / 200g granulated sugar
2 sticks plus 7 tablespoons / 331g unsalted butter, at cool room temperature and cut into small pieces
1 teaspoon grated blood orange zest (from 1 blood orange)
½ teaspoon vanilla extract
¼ teaspoon fine sea salt

BLOOD ORANGE GLAZE

3 tablespoons unsalted butter, melted
2 tablespoons heavy cream, at room temperature, plus more as needed
1½ cups / 180g powdered sugar, sifted
1 tablespoon freshly squeezed blood orange juice (from 1 blood orange), plus more as needed

ASSEMBLY

About ¾ cup / 195g Blood Orange Curd (recipe follows)
Small edible flowers with stems (see page 88), for decorating

1. FOR THE BLOOD ORANGE OLIVE OIL CAKE: Set a rack in the middle of the oven and preheat to 350°F / 180°C. Spray or brush the sides of one 8-inch / 20cm round cake pan with canola oil, then line the bottom with parchment paper.

2. Sift the flour, baking powder, and baking soda into a medium bowl. Add the salt.

3. In the bowl of a stand mixer, combine the granulated sugar and blood orange zest and use your fingers to massage the mixture, releasing the citrus oils.

4. In a small bowl, whisk together the blood orange juice and buttermilk.

5. Add the olive oil to the sugar and zest mixture, then use the paddle attachment to beat on medium speed until it's fully incorporated and the mixture looks like wet sand, about 30 seconds. Scrape the bottom and sides of the bowl, then add the eggs, one at a time, and beat on medium-low speed, scraping the bowl before each addition and again at the end, until fully incorporated. On low speed, add the flour mixture in three batches, alternating with the buttermilk mixture in two batches and scraping the bowl before each addition. Mix just

RECIPE CONTINUES

until there are no streaks. Scrape the bowl, then beat on medium speed for 30 seconds just to make sure the flour is fully incorporated. Do not overmix!

6. Pour the batter into the prepared pan, smoothing the top. Bake for 25 minutes, then quickly rotate the pan and continue baking until the top springs back when lightly pressed and a skewer inserted in the center comes out clean, 20 to 25 minutes.

7. Let the cake cool in the pan on a wire rack for 30 minutes. Carefully run a small offset spatula between the edges of the pan and the cake, then flip the pan onto the rack and tap it to make sure the cake is released. Remove the parchment paper. Use a second rack or a plate to flip the cake so it's right-side up on the rack. Let cool completely.

8. FOR THE BLOOD ORANGE SWISS MERINGUE BUTTERCREAM: (Before starting, read How to Make Swiss Meringue Buttercream, page 129.) Fill a medium saucepan with about 1 inch / 2.5cm of water and bring to a simmer over medium-low heat.

9. Use a paper towel and about ¼ teaspoon of white vinegar to wipe all over the surface of a large heatproof bowl and the bowl of a stand mixer, making sure there aren't any traces of liquid or fat.

10. In the clean heatproof bowl, combine the egg whites and granulated sugar, then set the bowl over the pan of simmering water, making sure the water does not touch the bottom of the bowl. Heat the mixture, whisking constantly, until it registers 130°F / 54°C on an instant-read thermometer, 3 to 4 minutes.

11. Transfer the mixture to the clean bowl of the stand mixer. Using the whisk attachment, whip on high speed until stiff peaks form, 8 to 10 minutes. Switch to the paddle attachment. Gradually start adding the butter in small batches and beat on medium-high speed, scraping the bowl as needed, until all the butter has been added. Beat on high speed until the buttercream is fluffy and has air bubbles, about 1 minute. Add the blood orange zest, vanilla, and salt and beat on low speed until fully combined, about 30 seconds.

12. FOR THE BLOOD ORANGE GLAZE: In a stand mixer fitted with the whisk, whip the melted butter and heavy cream on medium speed for 30 seconds. Add the powdered sugar in two batches and whip until fully combined, about 30 seconds per batch. Scrape the bowl, then add 1½ teaspoons of the juice and whip on high speed until fully incorporated, about 30 seconds. Scrape the bowl. The glaze should be a baby pink color. If the blood orange has a lot of pigment, you might not need to use more, but if the glaze isn't pink enough, add the remaining juice. If the glaze is too stiff, gradually add more heavy cream, ½ teaspoon at a time, and whip for another 30 seconds, until you achieve an even color and a thick spreadable glaze that is just slightly runny. If you prepare the glaze ahead, you may need to whip it to bring back the desired consistency.

13. TO ASSEMBLE: Place the cake, flat-side down, on a cake plate or stand.

14. Put about 2 cups / 320g of buttercream into a piping bag fitted with a plain round tip with a ½-inch / 13mm or similar diameter.

15. Holding the pastry tip about 1 inch / 2.5cm above the cake and starting at the edge of the cake, pipe a thick, rounded ring of buttercream around the perimeter. Spoon the blood orange curd into the middle and use a small offset spatula to spread it evenly.

16. Holding the pastry tip about 1 inch / 2.5cm above the cake and starting at the edge of the curd, start piping a spiral all the way into the center, with no gaps. Using a small offset spatula, gently spread the buttercream to connect the rings of the spiral together. Starting about ½ inch / 13mm in from the edge of the buttercream spiral, repeat the same process to create a second layer of buttercream. If you still have buttercream, add a third layer to give the dome more height. Use the small offset spatula to smooth the layers of buttercream into a rounded dome on top of the cake. Try to make the dome as smooth as possible.

17. Use a small offset spatula to spread a very thin layer of buttercream on the sides of the cake, all the way down to the bottom. With the small offset spatula or a bench scraper, try to make the buttercream as smooth as

RECIPE CONTINUES

BO CURD
3/29 KB

possible all the way around the cake. This will be a very thin crumb coat (see How to Assemble, Frost, and Cut a Layer Cake, page 53).

18. Put the cake in the refrigerator to chill and firm up the buttercream for 15 to 30 minutes.

19. Scoop about half of the glaze onto the dome of the chilled cake and with a small offset spatula gently spread it all over the top and sides to completely cover the cake and create the fondant-like effect. Add additional glaze to cover any patches. Put the cake back in the fridge for 15 minutes to firm up the buttercream and glaze.

20. Press the stems of the flowers into the cake (see Tips for Working with Flowers, page 85) and serve right away. The cake (without flowers) keeps covered in the refrigerator for up to 2 days. Remove the cake about 2 hours before serving, so the buttercream has time to soften.

Blood Orange Curd

MAKES 2 CUPS / 520G

17 ounces / 510g fresh raspberries (about 4 cups)
1 cup / 200g sugar
4 teaspoons grated blood orange zest (from 1 medium orange)
½ cup / 120ml freshly squeezed blood orange juice (from 2 medium oranges)
5 teaspoons cornstarch
210g egg yolks (about 14 large), at room temperature
1 stick plus 2 tablespoons / 150g unsalted butter, at room temperature and cut into small pieces
½ teaspoon fine sea salt

1. In a medium saucepan, combine the raspberries, sugar, blood orange zest, and blood orange juice. Cook the mixture over medium heat, stirring frequently and mashing the raspberries as you stir, until the sugar is dissolved and there are no chunks of raspberry, 5 to 10 minutes.

2. Pour through a fine-mesh sieve set over a medium bowl, pressing all the liquid out (discard the seeds and zest). Stir in the cornstarch, followed by the egg yolks, stirring vigorously to combine. Pour the mixture into a medium saucepan and cook over low heat, stirring constantly, until the curd thickens and coats the back of a spoon, about 5 minutes. It should register 170° to 180°F / 77° to 82°C on an instant-read thermometer.

3. Pour through a fine-mesh sieve set over a medium bowl. While the mixture is still hot, gradually but quickly whisk in the butter, one piece at a time, making sure the butter gets completely incorporated before adding the next piece. Whisk in the salt. If you want to seal the curd in jars for longer term storage, do so while it's still hot (see How to Can Jams and Curds, page 187).

4. Otherwise, press plastic wrap directly onto the surface of the curd to prevent a skin from forming and let cool for about 20 minutes, then refrigerate until cold. The curd keeps in an airtight container in the refrigerator for up to 7 days.

PISTACHIO PROSECCO CHERRY TIERED CAKE

MAKES ONE THREE-TIER CAKE (SERVES 32 TO 45)

I developed this recipe for my first-ever tiered wedding cake. It was for one of my earliest clients and the process was pretty terrifying, but as that was the start of my wedding cake making, I'll always cherish this recipe. The pistachio sponge has a light crumb that marries beautifully with the tanginess of the prosecco in the buttercream. I keep the cherry jam on the chunkier side to add some contrasting texture. For the sponge, the pistachios should be small enough to add crunch without making the cake heavy or oily.

The cake recipe is divided into two batches, with the first batch making the bottom tier, and the second batch making the middle and top tiers. It's best to bake your cakes a day in advance and keep them well wrapped and refrigerated or ideally frozen, which keeps them from drying out—allow 30 minutes for them to thaw slightly before assembling. If possible, assemble and decorate just before you want to present and serve the cake, but if you have room to refrigerate a fully assembled cake, you can assemble, decorate, and refrigerate the cake one day in advance—the flowers won't last longer than that. If you refrigerate the cake, take it out of the fridge about 2 hours before serving so the buttercream can soften.

PISTACHIO CAKE—BATCH ONE

- Canola oil spray or canola oil, for the pans
- 1¾ cups / 245g raw pistachios
- 3⅓ cups / 475g all-purpose flour
- 2 tablespoons baking powder
- 1½ teaspoons baking soda
- 1½ teaspoons fine sea salt
- 1 cup plus 2 tablespoons / 275g sour cream, at room temperature
- 1 cup plus 3 tablespoons / 275ml whole milk, at room temperature
- 1 stick plus 6 tablespoons / 198g unsalted butter, at room temperature
- 2½ cups / 500g sugar
- 3 tablespoons unsweetened pistachio paste
- 6 tablespoons / 90ml canola oil
- 1 tablespoon vanilla extract
- ¾ teaspoon almond extract
- 3 large eggs, at room temperature
- 1 large egg white, at room temperature

PISTACHIO CAKE—BATCH TWO

- 1 cup / 140g raw pistachios
- 1¾ cups / 245g all-purpose flour
- 1 tablespoon baking powder
- 2 teaspoons baking soda
- 1 teaspoon fine sea salt
- ½ cup plus 2 tablespoons / 150g sour cream, at room temperature
- ½ cup plus 1 tablespoon / 135ml whole milk, at room temperature
- 7 tablespoons / 105g unsalted butter, at room temperature
- 1¼ cups / 250g sugar
- 1 tablespoon unsweetened pistachio paste
- ¼ cup / 60ml canola oil
- 2 teaspoons vanilla extract
- ½ teaspoon almond extract
- 2 large eggs, at room temperature
- 1 large egg white, at room temperature

PROSECCO SWISS MERINGUE BUTTERCREAM

- 1¾ cups / 420ml prosecco
- Distilled white vinegar
- 490g egg whites (about 14 large), at room temperature
- 3½ cups / 700g sugar
- 10 sticks plus 5 tablespoons / 1.2kg unsalted butter, at cool room temperature and cut into small pieces
- 2 teaspoons champagne extract
- ¼ teaspoon fine sea salt

ASSEMBLY

- About 2¼ cups / 730g cherry jam, homemade (recipe follows) or store-bought
- Large and small flowers and greenery (see page 88), for decorating
- Dehydrated fruit slices (optional; page 103)
- Meringue Letters (optional; page 71), for decorating

1. **FOR THE PISTACHIO CAKE—BATCH ONE:** Set a rack in the middle of the oven and preheat to 350°F / 180°C. Spray or brush the sides of three 10-inch / 25cm round cake pans with canola oil, then line the bottoms with parchment paper.

2. In a food processor, pulse the pistachios until finely ground.

3. Sift the flour, baking powder, and baking soda into a large bowl. Add the ground pistachios and salt.

RECIPE CONTINUES

4. In a medium bowl, combine the sour cream and milk and whisk until fully combined.

5. In a stand mixer fitted with the paddle, beat the butter, sugar, and pistachio paste on medium-high speed until fully combined, creamy, and pale green, about 4 minutes. Scrape down the bottom and sides of the bowl, then add the canola oil and beat until the oil is fully incorporated and the batter is slightly fluffy, about 1 minute. Scrape the bowl, then add the vanilla and almond extracts. Add the whole eggs and egg white, one at a time, and beat, scraping the bowl before each addition and again at the end, until fully incorporated. On low speed, add the flour mixture in four batches, alternating with the sour cream mixture in three batches and scraping the bowl before each addition. Mix just until there are no streaks. Do not overmix! Scrape the bowl one final time to make sure the flour is fully incorporated.

6. Divide the batter evenly among the prepared pans, making sure you scrape all the batter from the bowl, then smooth the tops. Bake until the cakes are lightly golden on top and spongy when lightly pressed, 36 to 38 minutes.

7. Let the cakes cool in the pans on a wire rack for 30 minutes. Carefully run a small offset spatula between the edges of the pans and the cakes, then flip the pans onto the rack, and tap them to make sure the cakes are released. Remove the parchment paper. Use a second rack or a plate to flip the cakes so they are right-side up on the rack. Let cool completely.

8. FOR THE PISTACHIO CAKE—BATCH TWO: Repeat the steps for batch one to bake batch two but divide the batter among three 6-inch / 15cm round cake pans and two 4-inch / 10cm round cake pans. Bake the 6-inch / 15cm cakes for 32 to 34 minutes and the 4-inch / 10cm cakes for 30 to 32 minutes.

9. FOR THE PROSECCO SWISS MERINGUE BUTTERCREAM: (Before starting, read How to Make Swiss Meringue Buttercream, page 129.) In a small saucepan set over medium heat, bring the prosecco to a boil. Reduce the heat to medium-low and simmer until the prosecco is reduced by half, about 12 minutes. Remove from the heat and let cool to room temperature.

10. Fill a medium saucepan with about 1 inch / 2.5cm of water and bring to a simmer over medium-low heat.

11. Use a paper towel and about ¼ teaspoon of white vinegar to wipe all over the surface of a large heatproof bowl and the bowl of a stand mixer, making sure there aren't any traces of liquid or fat.

12. In the clean heatproof bowl, combine the egg whites and sugar, then set the bowl over the pan of simmering water, making sure the water does not touch the bottom of the bowl. Heat the mixture, whisking constantly, until it reaches 130°F / 54°C on an instant-read thermometer, 4 to 5 minutes.

13. Transfer to the clean bowl of the stand mixer. Using the whisk attachment, whip on high speed until stiff peaks form, about 10 minutes. Switch to the paddle attachment. Gradually start adding the butter in small batches and beat on medium-high speed, scraping the bowl as needed, until all the butter has been added. Add the cooled prosecco, champagne extract, and salt and beat on medium-high speed for 1 minute to incorporate. Increase the speed to high and beat until the buttercream is fluffy and has air bubbles, 3 to 4 minutes.

14. TO ASSEMBLE: Follow the instructions on How to Assemble a Tiered Cake (page 151) to finish the cake.

Cherry Jam

MAKES 4 CUPS / 1.3KG

3 pounds / 1.4kg pitted cherries, fresh or thawed frozen (about 10 cups), quartered
4 cups / 800g sugar
1 teaspoon fine sea salt
Juice of 2 lemons

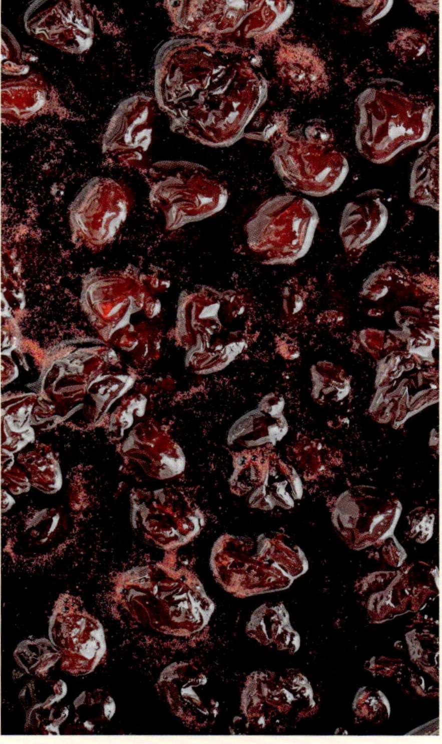

1. In a large bowl, combine the cherries and sugar and toss to coat the fruit. Cover and let macerate at room temperature for 2 hours or refrigerate overnight.

2. Put two small plates in the freezer.

3. Transfer the cherry mixture to a large Dutch oven or heavy-bottomed saucepan and cook over medium-high heat, stirring frequently to keep the fruit from burning. Use a potato masher to gently crush the cherries. Using a large stainless steel spoon, skim off the reddish pink foam that rises to the top as the mixture comes to a boil.

4. Continue cooking until the jam starts to feel a bit thick, then scoop a spoonful onto one of the frozen plates and wait 1 to 2 minutes for it to come to room temperature. Tip the plate from side to side. If the jam is ready, it will hold its shape on the plate rather than run down it. If you're not sure, try running a spoon through the jam on the plate—if it holds the line, it's ready. Technically, jam should register about 220°F / 104°C, and if you're new to jam making, using a thermometer can be really helpful, but part of the fun is relying on your senses. The jam should have a smooth texture studded with cherry skins and little chunks of fruit. If needed, continue cooking the jam until it sets on the second frozen plate.

5. Once the jam passes the plate test, add the salt and lemon juice, then remove it from the heat. If you want to seal the jam in jars for longer term storage, do so while it's still hot (see How to Can Jams and Curds, page 187).

6. Otherwise, let the jam stand in the pot, without stirring, to cool and thicken for about 30 minutes, then transfer it to jars or airtight containers but do not cover. Let the jam cool to room temperature, then cover and refrigerate for up to 2 weeks. You can cool the jam in the refrigerator, but it's important to allow the jam to fully cool before covering, as condensation could drip back into your beautiful work and loosen the texture.

How to

ASSEMBLE A TIERED CAKE

ASSEMBLING THE TIERS

TRIM THE LAYERS

Once the cake layers are cool, using a serrated knife and starting about 1 inch / 2.5cm in from the edge, carefully trim the tops to make them flat.

ASSEMBLE THE FIRST TIER

Place one of the 10-inch / 25cm cakes, flat-side down, on a 12-inch / 30.5cm cardboard cake round or plate.

Put about 1½ cups / 300g of the buttercream into a piping bag fitted with a plain round tip with a ½-inch / 13mm or similar diameter.

Holding the pastry tip about 1 inch / 2.5cm above the cake and starting about ¼ inch / 6mm from the edge of the cake, pipe 2 concentric rounded rings of buttercream around the perimeter. Spoon ½ to ¾ cup / 165 to 245g of jam or curd into the center and use a small offset spatula to spread it evenly. Pipe zigzags of buttercream on top of the jam or curd so it's completely covered. Using a small offset spatula, gently spread the buttercream zigzags to fill in any gaps and connect them to the outer rings of buttercream, while leaving them intact.

Carefully place a second 10-inch / 25cm cake, flat-side down, on top, then gently wiggle it into the buttercream. Add more buttercream to the piping bag and repeat the above process to add buttercream and jam or curd to this layer.

Carefully place the third 10-inch / 25cm cake, flat-side up, on top, then gently wiggle it into the buttercream. Add more buttercream to the piping bag and repeat the above process, but pipe the rings of buttercream on the edge of the cake and skip the jam or curd (see How to Assemble, Frost, and Cut a Layer Cake, page 53).

If the top of the cake isn't even, add a small amount of buttercream under the layers to help level it. Once the cake tier is assembled, refrigerate it to firm up before stacking.

ASSEMBLE THE SECOND TIER

Place one of the 6-inch / 15cm cakes, flat-side down, on a 5-inch / 13cm cardboard cake round.

Put about 2¼ cups / 340g of the buttercream into a piping bag fitted with a plain round tip with a ½-inch / 13mm or similar diameter. Repeat the process as for the first tier, but using the 6-inch / 15cm cakes, about ¼ cup / 80g of jam or curd between the layers, and ¾ cup / 115g of buttercream between each layer and on top. Once the cake tier is assembled, refrigerate it to firm up before stacking.

ASSEMBLE THE THIRD TIER

Place one of the 4-inch / 10cm cakes, flat-side down, on a 3-inch / 7.5cm cardboard cake round.

Put about ½ cup / 75g of buttercream into a piping bag fitted with a plain round tip with a ½-inch / 13mm or similar diameter. This tier has only two layers, but the process is the same, just skip the middle layer and use about 3 tablespoons of jam or curd between the layers and ¼ cup / 40g of buttercream between the two layers and on top. Once the cake tier is assembled, refrigerate it to firm up before stacking.

STACKING THE TIERS

Take the 10-inch / 25cm cake tier out of the refrigerator. Measure 2½ inches / 6cm from the center of the cake, then place a wooden dowel in that spot and carefully push it straight down through the cake layers. Use a nontoxic edible marker to mark the dowel where it meets the top of the cake. Remove the dowel and cut it to size, using your mark (or the buttercream line).

Repeat this process to cut 3 more dowels, arranging the holes so they are equidistant from each other, and all 2½ inches / 6cm from the center of the cake so you could draw a circle to connect them. Once the dowels are cut, place them in the holes and refrigerate the cake tier.

Take the 6-inch / 15cm cake tier out of the refrigerator. Repeat the dowel measuring and cutting process but use only 2 dowels and place them each about 1 inch / 2.5cm from the center of the cake and on opposite sides of the cake for balance. Once the dowels are cut, place them in the holes.

Take the 10-inch / 25cm cake tier out of the refrigerator. Carefully stack the 6-inch / 15cm cake tier on top, centering it precisely. Take the 4-inch / 10cm cake tier out of the refrigerator and carefully stack it on top of the 6-inch / 15cm cake tier, centering it precisely.

DECORATING AND FINISHING TOUCHES

Arrange a few large flowers and greenery on top of the cake, then fill in any remaining gaps with small flowers (see Tips for Working with Flowers, page 85). Add dehydrated fruit slices and sprinkle crushed pistachios and freeze-dried raspberries on the buttercream, if desired. Add meringue letters, if desired (see How to Decorate Cakes, page 83.)

The cake (without foliage) keeps covered in the refrigerator for up to 2 days. Remove the cake about 2 hours before serving, so the buttercream has time to soften.

DESSERT

Whimsical Takes on Classic Desserts

CHERRY CLAFOUTIS

MAKES ONE 9-INCH / 23CM CLAFOUTIS

In our garden when I was growing up, we had this incredible cherry tree with a sturdy playhouse, built by my dad, nestled in its branches. The tree also produced an endless number of cherries each summer.

When I make clafoutis, I like to stick to tradition by leaving the pits in the cherries. It may sound unconventional, but the pits preserve more juice and deepen the cherry flavor as it bakes. And then there's the joy of savoring each bite, sucking on the pits for that extra burst of cherry before elegantly spitting them out—it's all part of the experience!

This recipe works beautifully with sweet or tart cherries, but make sure they're perfectly ripe. Choose a pie dish with high sides to give the custardy batter room to puff up and envelop the cherries as it bakes. Whether it's a taste of nostalgia or a new family favorite, this clafoutis is all about celebrating cherries in their purest form.

Softened unsalted butter, for the pie dish
¾ cup / 150g sugar
¾ cup plus 1 tablespoon / 195ml whole milk
¼ cup / 60ml heavy cream
¾ cup / 105g all-purpose flour
⅛ teaspoon fine sea salt
4 large eggs, at room temperature
1 teaspoon vanilla extract
5 tablespoons / 75g unsalted butter, melted
17 ounces / 510g ripe cherries (3½ to 4 cups)

1. Set a rack in the lower third of the oven and preheat to 400°F / 200°C. Butter a 9-inch / 23cm ceramic or glass pie dish with sides that are at least 1½ inches / 4cm tall. Sprinkle ¼ cup / 50g of the sugar all over the surface of the buttered pie dish.

2. In a small saucepan, bring the milk and heavy cream to a simmer over medium heat. Remove from the heat.

3. In a large bowl, whisk together the flour, salt, and remaining ½ cup / 100g sugar.

4. In a small bowl, whisk together the eggs and vanilla, then add to the flour mixture. Whisk vigorously until thick and pale, 1 to 2 minutes. Scrape down the bottom and sides of the bowl, then gradually add the melted butter, followed by the warm milk mixture, and whisk until uniform, about 1 minute. The batter will be quite thin.

5. Spread the cherries evenly on the bottom of the prepared pie dish, then pour the batter over the cherries. Bake for 10 minutes, then reduce the oven temperature to 350°F / 180°C and continue baking until the clafoutis is golden on top and has a firm, slightly custard-like texture, about 45 minutes. It will puff up a little on the sides but quickly deflate once it's out of the oven.

6. Set the pie dish on a wire rack and let the clafoutis cool for 30 minutes. Serve lukewarm or cold, straight from the pie dish. Clafoutis is best enjoyed the day it's baked, but it keeps covered in the refrigerator for up to 3 days.

MENSUEL FRANCE 13,50 F - BELGIQUE 120 FB

CHOCOLATE MINT MOUSSE

SERVES ABOUT 10

As a child, I used to dream about eating rich, creamy, dark chocolate mousse. I've always loved the deepest, darkest chocolate, even back then. I've added a twist to this childhood favorite, with a cool, refreshing hint of mint. It adds a light, digestive quality that makes this mousse the perfect end to a heavy meal, much like an after-dinner mint, my father's preferred treat. While I love pairing chocolate and mint, you can experiment with other fresh herbs, like rosemary or thyme, for your own unique spin.

The secret to truly great mousse lies in the details. Start with the best chocolate, preferably 72% cacao or higher for that intense, velvety flavor. Use the freshest eggs, ideally less than six days old, and let them come to room temperature for at least 1 hour. Fresh mint is a must, as extract has a toothpaste-like flavor, and you'll miss out on the true essence of the herb. Allow plenty of time for the mousse to chill in the fridge, so each spoonful is silky, airy, and packed with flavor.

1 stick plus 1 tablespoon / 128g unsalted butter, cut into small pieces
6 sprigs fresh mint, leaves roughly chopped and stems discarded
7 ounces / 200g dark chocolate, preferably 72% cacao, chopped
Distilled white vinegar
8 large eggs, separated
3 tablespoons sugar
⅛ teaspoon fine sea salt
Maldon sea salt, for sprinkling

1. In a small saucepan, melt the butter over medium-low heat. Remove from the heat, then stir in the mint, cover, and let stand for 30 minutes.

2. Pour through a fine-mesh sieve set over a small bowl, pressing on the mint to extract as much flavor as possible (discard the mint).

3. Fill a medium saucepan with about 1 inch / 2.5cm of water and bring to a simmer over medium-low heat. In a large heatproof bowl, combine the mint-infused butter and the chocolate, then set the bowl over the pan of simmering water, making sure the water does not touch the bottom of the bowl. Warm the mixture, stirring occasionally, until the chocolate is melted and fully combined with the butter. Remove the bowl from the pan (careful—it will be warm!) and use a clean kitchen towel to carefully wipe any condensation from the bottom of the bowl.

4. Meanwhile, use a paper towel and about ¼ teaspoon of white vinegar to wipe all over the surface of the bowl of a stand mixer, making sure there aren't any traces of liquid or fat.

5. In the clean bowl of the stand mixer fitted with the whisk, whip the egg whites on high speed until soft peaks form, 3 to 5 minutes.

6. In a large bowl, whisk the egg yolks and 4 teaspoons of the sugar vigorously until pale and aerated, 2 to 3 minutes.

7. Once the chocolate is melted and combined with the butter, pour it over the egg yolk mixture and whisk until fully combined. Add the salt and whisk to incorporate.

8. Once the egg whites are at soft peaks, add the remaining sugar and whip on high speed until stiff peaks form, 7 to 8 minutes. If you're unsure if the meringue is stiff peak, remove the whisk attachment from the stand mixer and flip it so it's whisk-side up. The peaks should point straight up and be very stiff. Add about one-third of the whipped egg whites to the chocolate and egg yolk mixture and whisk until incorporated. Add the remaining egg whites and gently fold with a rubber spatula until fully incorporated and uniform in color. Transfer the mousse to a serving bowl, cover, and refrigerate for at least 4 hours or preferably overnight.

9. Sprinkle with the Maldon salt and serve! The mousse keeps covered in the refrigerator for up to 2 days.

MINI PAVLOVAS

MAKES 6 TO 8 MINI PAVLOVAS

This recipe comes straight from my mother, who is from New Zealand. I love making mini pavlovas. Not only do they look impressive, but they're also much easier to plate. The key to a perfect pavlova is getting your meringue stiff enough before baking. If you can hold the bowl upside down without the meringue moving, you're good to go. When baked, the pavlovas should have a delicate, crackly exterior and a soft center. To finish, use the best fruit you can find, and top it with crème fraîche for a subtle tang that balances the sweetness. It's a little slice of home that I never get tired of sharing.

Distilled white vinegar
140g egg whites (about 4 large), at room temperature
1¼ cups / 250g sugar
4 teaspoons cornstarch
1 teaspoon apple cider vinegar
1 teaspoon vanilla extract
Crème fraîche, for serving
8 small apricots, pitted and quartered, for serving
Small edible flowers (see page 88), for decorating

1. Set a rack in the middle of the oven and preheat to 225°F / 110°C. Line the bottom of one 13 × 18-inch / 33 × 45cm or similarly sized baking sheet with parchment paper.

2. Use a paper towel and about ¼ teaspoon of white vinegar to wipe all over the surface of the bowl of a stand mixer, making sure there aren't any traces of liquid or fat.

3. In the clean bowl of the stand mixer fitted with the whisk, whip the egg whites on medium-high speed until stiff peaks form, 3 to 4 minutes. Gradually add the sugar. Continue whipping for 3 to 4 minutes, then increase the speed to high and whip until very stiff peaks form, about 1 minute. Add the cornstarch, apple cider vinegar, and vanilla and gently fold with a rubber spatula until just incorporated.

4. Set a 3-inch / 7.5cm metal baking ring on the prepared baking sheet. Use a spoon to fill the ring all the way to the top with the meringue mixture, then use the spoon to create swoops on the top of the pavlova. Run a small, thin knife along the inside of the ring to release the pavlova, then quickly pull the ring directly upward to create tiny peaks along the edges of the pavlova. Repeat to make 5 to 7 more pavlovas.

5. Bake for 1 hour, then turn the oven off and let the pavlovas set and dry out in the oven while it cools for another hour. Do not open the oven door! The pavlovas should be crunchy on the outside but soft and tender on the inside.

6. Serve the pavlovas topped with crème fraîche, apricots, and flowers or petals. Pavlovas (without toppings) keep in an airtight container at room temperature for up to 1 week.

RASPBERRY CHEESECAKE SWIRLED BROWNIES

MAKES 15 BROWNIES

My mum used to bake these when I was growing up, and they've always been the perfect afternoon treat—a brighter, fruitier take on classic brownies. Cream cheese gives them a lovely lightness, while raspberries cut through the sweetness with just enough sharpness. The marble effect of the swirled chocolate and cream cheese creates a beautiful, swishy pattern that makes these even more irresistible. It's the sort of recipe you simply have to try. At the bakery, we always trim the edges to make the brownies look neat and tidy—and somehow, we end up devouring every last one of those offcuts.

Softened unsalted butter, for the pan
7 ounces / 200g dark chocolate, chopped
1 stick plus 6 tablespoons / 198g unsalted butter, at room temperature
2 cups / 400g sugar
5 large eggs, at room temperature
¾ cup plus 1 tablespoon / 115g all-purpose flour
1¾ cups plus 1 tablespoon / 400g cream cheese, at room temperature and cut into small pieces
1 teaspoon vanilla extract
1 cup / 120g raspberries, fresh or frozen (not thawed)

1. Set a rack in the middle of the oven and preheat to 350°F / 180°C. Lightly butter the bottom and sides of a 9 × 13-inch / 23 × 33cm metal baking pan, then line the pan with parchment paper, leaving about 1 inch / 2.5cm hanging over the sides.

2. Fill a medium saucepan with about 1 inch / 2.5cm of water and bring to a simmer over medium-low heat. Add the chocolate to a large heatproof bowl and set the bowl over the pan of simmering water, making sure the water does not touch the bottom of the bowl. Warm the chocolate, stirring occasionally, until melted. Remove the bowl from the pan (careful—it will be warm!) and use a clean kitchen towel to carefully wipe any condensation from the bottom of the bowl. Set aside to cool.

3. In a stand mixer fitted with the paddle, beat the butter and 1 cup / 200g of the sugar on medium-high speed, scraping down the bottom and sides of the bowl as needed, until pale and fluffy, about 2 minutes. Scrape the bowl, then add 3 of the eggs, one at a time, and beat, scraping the bowl before each addition and again at the end, until fully incorporated. Add the cooled chocolate and mix on low speed until fully incorporated.

4. Remove the bowl from the stand mixer, then gradually add the flour, gently folding with a rubber spatula, just until there are no streaks. The batter will be quite thick.

5. Spread about three-quarters of the batter in the prepared pan, smoothing the top. Set the rest aside.

6. In the clean bowl of a stand mixer fitted with a clean paddle, beat the cream cheese and the remaining 1 cup / 200g sugar on medium-high speed until it has the texture of whipped cream cheese, about 2 minutes. Scrape the bowl, then add the remaining 2 eggs and the vanilla and beat, scraping the bowl as needed, until smooth, about 1 minute.

7. Spread this mixture over the batter in the pan, smoothing the top but maintaining the distinct layers. Dollop the reserved chocolate batter over the cream cheese mixture and use a fork to swirl them together. Push the raspberries into the top.

8. Bake until a skewer inserted in the center comes out mostly clean with just a few moist crumbs, 45 to 50 minutes.

9. Let the brownies cool completely in the pan on a wire rack. Carefully wiggle the parchment paper to release the brownies from the pan, then lift the parchment and use it to place the brownies on a cutting board. Cut into equal squares for serving. The brownies keep in an airtight container in the refrigerator for up to 5 days, or can be well wrapped and frozen for up to 2 months.

PRIDE AND PREJUDICE
ALEX GARLAND
Gabrielle Roy
The Tin Flute
ANGELICA GARNETT
Deceived with Kindness

RHUBARB GINGER CRUMBLE

SERVES 6

Crumbles tend not to be the most aesthetically pleasing desserts, but oh my, are they one of the best tasting. This rhubarb and ginger combo is one of my favorites, as the spice of the ginger adds depth and warmth to the rhubarb, which can be a bit flat on its own. Pair with some cold crème anglaise and you'll be sure to wow your guests—or just yourself!

Though this recipe is simple, it does require refrigerating the rhubarb and sugar for 3 hours. This allows the sugar crystals to fully dissolve and mingle with the rhubarb, creating a vibrant, flavorful syrup at the bottom of the bowl—leftover syrup is perfect for sweetening lemonade.

1½ pounds / 680g chopped rhubarb
1 cup / 200g granulated sugar
¾ cup / 105g all-purpose flour
3 tablespoons almond flour
6 tablespoons / 75g (packed) dark brown sugar
Pinch of fine sea salt
6 tablespoons / 90g unsalted butter, cut into small pieces
Softened unsalted butter, for the baking dish
2 tablespoons finely grated peeled fresh ginger (from a 1-inch / 2.5cm piece)
Rose Crème Anglaise (recipe follows), chilled, or cold crème fraîche, for serving

1. In a medium bowl, combine the rhubarb and granulated sugar and toss to coat. Cover and refrigerate, stirring every hour, for 3 hours.

2. Meanwhile, in a large bowl, whisk together the flours, brown sugar, and salt. Add the butter and use your hands to work it into the mixture until it has a slightly sticky and sandy texture with a mix of smaller and larger crumbles. Cover and refrigerate for at least 30 minutes, or until ready to use.

3. When ready to bake, set a rack in the middle of the oven and preheat to 400°F / 200°C. Generously butter the bottom and sides of a 9-inch / 23cm square ceramic or glass baking dish.

4. Using a slotted spoon, scoop the rhubarb into a medium saucepan, then add about 2 tablespoons of the liquid from the bowl (reserve the remaining liquid). Set the saucepan over low heat, cover, and cook, stirring occasionally until the rhubarb is slightly soft but not mushy, about 15 minutes. If the pan gets too dry, add more of the reserved liquid, 1 tablespoon at a time.

5. Use the slotted spoon to transfer the rhubarb to a medium bowl, leaving any extra juice in the saucepan. Add the ginger to the bowl and toss gently but thoroughly with the rhubarb.

6. Spread the rhubarb mixture in the prepared baking dish and sprinkle the cold crumble mixture on top. Don't press it down. Bake until the crumble is golden, about 30 minutes.

7. Set the dish on a wire rack and let the crumble cool slightly. Serve warm or cold with a side of cold rose crème anglaise or crème fraîche.

Rose Crème Anglaise

MAKES 2 CUPS / 480ML

2 cups plus 2 tablespoons / 510ml whole milk
⅓ cup / 5g dried organic rose petals, plus more for serving
⅛ teaspoon fine sea salt
4 large egg yolks
⅓ cup / 65g sugar

1. In a small saucepan, warm the milk over low heat just until steam starts to rise from the surface; do not let it come to a simmer or bubble. Remove from the heat, then stir in the rose petals. Let the mixture steep, uncovered and at room temperature, for 30 minutes. Transfer to a small bowl, cover, and refrigerate for at least 2 hours but preferably overnight.

2. Pour through a fine-mesh sieve set over a medium saucepan, pressing on the petals to extract as much flavor as possible (discard the petals). The milk will be a very light brown color. Add the salt and set the pan over low heat to warm just until steam starts to rise from the surface; do not let it come to a simmer or bubble.

3. Meanwhile, in a heatproof medium bowl, vigorously whisk the egg yolks and the sugar until fully combined and lighter in color.

4. Remove the hot milk from the heat and while stirring constantly with a wooden spoon, very gradually add it to the egg yolk mixture. Pour the mixture back into the saucepan, set it over medium-low heat, and warm it, stirring frequently, until the small bubbles disappear and the mixture thickens and becomes opaque on the spoon. Do not let it boil. One way to know if it's ready is to coat your spoon with the mixture and run your finger over it. If the line is neat, then it's ready. A more precise way to know is if the mixture is about 185°F / 85°C. It will thicken as it sits.

5. Pour through a fine-mesh sieve set over a serving bowl and let stand at room temperature for 20 minutes, stirring every 5 minutes to prevent a skin from forming. You will end up with a light brown cream. Cover and refrigerate until cold, about 1 hour. Whisk before serving and sprinkle with dried rose petals for decoration. The crème anglaise keeps in an airtight container in the refrigerator for up to 2 days. Make sure to whisk it before serving.

TIRAMISU CHARLOTTE

MAKES ONE 9-INCH / 23CM CAKE

During my undergrad years, I had the privilege of studying art history in Rome, and like any good student there, I spent my time eating cacio e pepe, enjoying gelato, sipping spritzes, and, of course, indulging in tiramisu.

I've always loved the taste of tiramisu, but I found it hard to serve—its layered structure and the mess of cutting into it never quite worked for me. At the same time, I've always admired the look of a classic French charlotte, though I've never been a fan of the crème bavaroise filling, and I'm not keen on working with gelatin. So, I decided to bring together what I think are the best parts of each one into what, honestly, is one of my favorite desserts.

When piping the ladyfinger biscuit discs, be sure to make them just slightly smaller than the pan you're using, so they fit neatly in the center without breaking. While store-bought ladyfingers will work—you can arrange them to create the discs—homemade ones offer a softness and flavor that really take this dessert to the next level.

LADYFINGER BISCUITS

1 cup plus 1 tablespoon / 150g all-purpose flour
6 large eggs, separated and at room temperature
¾ cup / 150g granulated sugar
Powdered sugar, for dusting

MASCARPONE FILLING

4 large eggs, separated and at room temperature
¾ cup plus 2 tablespoons / 175g granulated sugar
1¾ cups / 400g mascarpone

ASSEMBLY

1⅓ cups / 320ml brewed espresso, cooled
1 tablespoon plus ¼ teaspoon amaretto or coffee liqueur
Unsweetened Dutch-process cocoa powder, for dusting

1. FOR THE LADYFINGER BISCUITS: Set the racks in the upper and lower thirds of the oven and preheat to 350°F / 180°C. Line two 13 × 18-inch / 33 × 45cm or similarly sized baking sheets with parchment paper.

2. Sift the flour into a small bowl.

3. In a stand mixer fitted with the whisk, whip the egg whites on medium-high speed until foamy, about 2 minutes. On high speed, gradually add half of the granulated sugar. Continue whipping until stiff peaks start to form, then gradually add the remaining granulated sugar and whip until very stiff peaks form. Quickly add the egg yolks and whip on medium speed for a few seconds just until combined.

4. Remove the bowl from the stand mixer. Gently fold in the flour in two batches with a rubber spatula, being careful to not deflate the mixture, just until incorporated.

5. Transfer the batter to a piping bag fitted with a plain round tip with a ½-inch / 13mm or similar diameter.

6. On one prepared baking sheet, pipe two rows of 7 oblong-shaped 3-inch / 7.5cm long ladyfinger biscuits, piping them so they are side-by-side in a line and touching on their longer sides. These will form the sides of your charlotte, so it's important to pipe them so they are completely joined along their sides.

7. On the second prepared baking sheet, pipe 3 discs 8 inches / 20cm in diameter. To do this, start on the outside edge of where the disc will be and pipe a spiral until you reach the center with no gaps between the lines. Repeat two more times. These discs will be the base and layers of your charlotte.

8. Lightly dust all the biscuits with powdered sugar. Bake until lightly golden, 10 to 12 minutes.

9. Set the pans on a wire rack, dust the biscuits with more powdered sugar, and let cool completely.

10. FOR THE MASCARPONE FILLING: In a stand mixer fitted with the whisk, whip the egg whites on high speed until stiff peaks form, 4 to 5 minutes. Transfer to a clean bowl. Do not clean the stand mixer bowl.

RECIPE CONTINUES

11. In the stand mixer fitted with the paddle, beat the egg yolks and granulated sugar on medium-high speed until pale and thick, about 5 minutes. Add the mascarpone and beat on medium speed until smooth and fully incorporated, 1 to 2 minutes.

12. Remove the bowl from the stand mixer. Add the whipped egg whites and gently fold with a rubber spatula until incorporated, being careful to maintain the airy texture.

13. TO ASSEMBLE: Place a 9-inch / 23cm cake ring with 3-inch / 7.5cm sides (or a springform pan without the base) on a serving plate. Line the interior walls with the cooled strips of oblong-shaped ladyfinger biscuits, trimming them to fit as needed. Place one of the round ladyfinger discs on the plate to form the base of the charlotte.

14. In a wide, shallow bowl, combine the espresso and amaretto. Use a pastry brush to generously brush this mixture onto the ladyfinger base and sides. Repeat two more times to thoroughly soak the ladyfingers. Spread one-third of the mascarpone filling over the biscuit base, smoothing the top. Dust with cocoa powder.

15. Soak another ladyfinger disc in the espresso mixture, flipping to soak both sides, then place it on top of the mascarpone filling. Add half of the remaining mascarpone filling, spread it evenly, then dust with cocoa powder. Soak the remaining ladyfinger disc, then place it on top. Top with the remaining mascarpone filling, spread it evenly, and generously dust the top with more cocoa powder.

16. Refrigerate the assembled charlotte overnight to allow the flavors to meld and the mixture to set.

17. Carefully slide the cake ring (or springform pan ring) upward to remove it, then dust the charlotte with more cocoa powder, slice, and serve cold. The charlotte keeps covered in the refrigerator for up to 3 days.

APPLE QUINCE COMPOTE

SERVES 8

In France, applesauce—we call it compote—is a cherished dish for adults and children alike, and we even have a special vessel for it called a compotière. Adding quince and a touch of star anise elevates the flavors, lending a beautiful citrusy brightness and subtle licorice notes. I love presenting compote in the apple skins, turning them into natural "jars," but a simple bowl works just as well. If you do use the apples as jars, prepare them the day of serving to prevent the skins from turning too soft. Leave the apple vessels empty until you're ready to serve, then fill them with the compote at the last minute to maintain their structure.

8 ripe apples, preferably Fuji, with stems attached
Juice of 1 lemon
4 ripe quinces
¾ cup plus 1 tablespoon / 160g (packed) light brown sugar
14 star anise pods
1 teaspoon vanilla bean paste
½ teaspoon fine sea salt
4 teaspoons unsalted butter

1. Carefully cut the top ¼ to ½ inch / 6 to 13mm off the top of each apple. Set these apple "hats" aside.

2. Using a small knife, a metal teaspoon, or a melon baller, carefully cut a small hole in the center of each apple to remove as much of the core as possible without cutting all the way through to the bottom. You need to keep the bottoms intact, so don't use an apple corer for this step. Carefully scoop out the insides of the apples. Try to scoop out as much flesh as possible without breaking the skin. Add all of the scooped-out apple flesh to a large saucepan.

3. Use a small pastry brush to brush the lemon juice all over the insides of the apples and on the bottom surfaces of the apple hats.

4. Peel the quinces and cut each into quarters. Remove the cores and seeds, then cut the flesh into roughly ½-inch / 13mm pieces. Add the quince to the saucepan with the apple flesh. Add the brown sugar, star anise, vanilla bean paste, salt, and 2 tablespoons water. Set the pan over medium heat and cook, stirring, until the sugar is dissolved. Turn the heat to low, cover, and cook for 20 minutes.

5. Remove the star anise, then turn the heat to medium and cook, stirring and gently mashing the fruit on the sides of the pan, until the fruit is soft, about 5 minutes. Remove from the heat, then add the butter and stir until melted and incorporated.

6. Transfer the mixture to a blender and process until smooth with no chunks. Let the compote cool slightly, then cover it with plastic wrap and refrigerate until cold.

7. When ready to serve, fill the emptied apples (or small bowls) with the compote and cover with the apple hats. The compote can be served cold or at room temperature. The compote (without the apple "jars") keeps in an airtight container in the refrigerator for up to 4 days.

PEAR ALMOND CHOCOLATE TART

MAKES ONE 9-INCH / 23CM TART

While I like to indulge in tarts, the idea of making one always felt a bit daunting. That all changed with this recipe. All the pastry dough ingredients go in the stand mixer at once, and this pastry is really easy to roll out. It's also versatile enough to adapt to all your needs—simply omit the cocoa powder for a traditional tart crust or skip the cocoa powder and sugar for savory applications like quiche. While you can roll out the pastry immediately, I recommend chilling it first, as it makes handling and shaping so much easier.

This tart brings together three of my favorite flavors: chocolate, almond, and pear. The pears, with their elegant shape, lend a touch of whimsy to the presentation, while also adding a soft, melt-in-your-mouth texture that pairs beautifully with rich dark chocolate and nutty almonds. To ensure the best results, choose pears that are ripe but still firm enough to hold their shape during baking.

TART PASTRY

1½ cups plus 1 tablespoon / 220g all-purpose flour
¼ cup / 50g sugar
2 tablespoons unsweetened Dutch-process cocoa powder, sifted
¼ teaspoon fine sea salt
7 tablespoons / 105g unsalted butter, at room temperature and cut into small pieces
2 large egg yolks, at room temperature

POACHED PEARS

¾ cup / 150g sugar
Juice of 1 lemon
4 Bosc pears with long stems

CHOCOLATE ALMOND FILLING

3½ ounces / 100g dark chocolate, chopped
1 stick plus 3 tablespoons / 143g unsalted butter, at room temperature
½ cup / 100g sugar
1 large egg, at room temperature
2 teaspoons almond extract
½ teaspoon fine sea salt
2 cups / 200g almond flour

1. FOR THE TART PASTRY: In a stand mixer fitted with the paddle, beat the all-purpose flour, sugar, cocoa powder, salt, butter, egg yolks, and 3 tablespoons water on medium speed until the butter is fully incorporated and the pastry is smooth and homogenous, about 2 minutes. Wrap the pastry in plastic wrap and refrigerate for at least 1 hour. The pastry can also be well wrapped and refrigerated for up to 2 days; if it's too firm to roll out, let it sit at room temperature for 30 minutes before rolling.

2. On a floured surface, use a floured rolling pin to roll out the pastry into a roughly ⅛-inch / 3mm thick round. Carefully roll it up and around the rolling pin and transfer it to a 9-inch / 23cm fluted metal tart pan with a removable bottom. Using floured fingers, gently press the pastry evenly into the tart pan, making sure it fits into the curves of the pan. Roll the rolling pin over the top of the pie dish to remove any excess pastry, then use a fork to poke holes all over the bottom of the tart shell. Chill in the fridge for 10 minutes.

3. Set a rack in the middle of the oven and preheat the oven to 350°F / 180°C.

4. Line the chilled tart shell with parchment paper, then fill it with pie weights or dried beans. Bake for 10 minutes.

5. Set the pan on a wire rack, carefully remove the pie weights or dried beans and parchment paper (they'll be hot!), and let the tart shell cool while you make the filling. Keep the oven on.

6. FOR THE POACHED PEARS: In a medium saucepan, bring the sugar, lemon juice, and 4½ cups / 1L water to a simmer over medium heat.

7. Meanwhile, peel the pears, keeping the stems attached. Once the poaching liquid is simmering, add the pears and simmer until tender, about 15 minutes. Remove from the heat and let the pears cool in their poaching liquid.

8. **FOR THE CHOCOLATE ALMOND FILLING:** Fill a medium saucepan with about 1 inch / 2.5cm of water and bring to a simmer over low heat. Add the chocolate to a large heatproof bowl, then set the bowl over the pan of simmering water, making sure the water does not touch the bottom of the bowl. Warm the chocolate, stirring, until melted. Remove the bowl from the pan (careful—it will be warm!) and use a clean kitchen towel to carefully wipe any condensation from the bottom of the bowl. Let cool.

9. In a stand mixer fitted with the paddle, beat the butter and sugar on medium-high speed, scraping down the bottom and sides of the bowl as needed, until creamy, about 1 minute. Scrape the bowl, then add the egg and beat until fully incorporated, about 2 minutes. The mixture may look slightly curdled. Add the almond extract, salt, and the cooled chocolate and beat until combined and creamy, about 1 minute. Scrape the bowl, then add the almond flour and beat on medium-low speed, scraping the bowl as needed, just until the mixture is evenly brown and has a paste-like texture, about 30 seconds.

10. Spoon about two-thirds of the chocolate almond filling into the cooled tart shell, spreading it into an even layer.

11. Using the stems, carefully remove the pears from the poaching liquid (discard the liquid). Cut the pears horizontally in half, making sure the stems stay attached to the top halves. Set the top halves aside.

12. Cut the bottom halves of the pears in half, then remove the seeds and cores and cut the fruit into small cubes. Press the cubes into the chocolate almond filling in the tart shell. Spoon the remaining chocolate almond filling on top, spreading it to completely cover the pears and create an even layer. Holding them carefully by their stems, place the top halves of the pears on top of the filling, pressing them gently so they are slightly submerged in the filling and standing up straight.

13. Bake until the chocolate almond filling puffs up and a skewer inserted in the center of the tart, between the pears, comes out with wet crumbs—it shouldn't be gooey—1 hour to 1 hour 10 minutes.

14. Set the pan on a wire rack and let the tart cool completely. Serve at room temperature. The tart keeps covered in the refrigerator for up to 3 days.

Pièce Montée
Pâte à choux
Sauce Demi-glace
Jus Brun
Vin de Framboise
Ingredients
Bake for 1h.
DRIED APRICOT JAM
DRIED APRICOT AND PINEAPPLE JAM
Marmelade (very good recepy)
Prune Chutney

LAVENDER RICE PUDDING

SERVES 8

Rice pudding is a personal favorite. Growing up, I ate homemade vanilla bean rice pudding every other week at my primary school. To me, rice pudding is all about that perfect creamy and soft rice—I add whipped cream at the end to really dial up the creaminess. I highly recommend putting your nose in the saucepan to smell the warmth of the sugar, milk, and lavender coming together. While it's not absolutely essential, sprinkling fresh lilac blossoms on top adds a bit of color and hints at the lavender flavor.

4½ cups / 1L whole milk
3 tablespoons dried culinary lavender
½ cup / 100g short-grain sushi rice
5 tablespoons / 75g sugar
⅛ teaspoon fine sea salt
¼ cup / 60ml heavy cream, cold
Small edible flowers (see page 88), for decorating

1. In a medium saucepan, combine the milk and lavender and gently stir to make sure the lavender is coated. Set the pan over medium heat and warm the mixture just until steam starts to rise from the surface; do not let it come to a simmer or bubble. Remove from the heat, cover, and let stand for 15 to 20 minutes.

2. Pour through a fine-mesh sieve set over a medium bowl, pressing on the lavender to extract as much flavor as possible (discard the lavender).

3. Pour the milk back into the medium saucepan and bring to a simmer. Add the rice, then turn the heat to low and simmer, stirring occasionally and briefly covering the saucepan every now and then to slow down the evaporation of the milk, until the rice is very soft and almost mushy, 45 to 50 minutes.

4. Remove from the heat, then add the sugar and salt and stir to incorporate. Let cool to room temperature.

5. Meanwhile, in a medium bowl, vigorously whisk the heavy cream until stiff peaks form, about 5 minutes.

6. Add the whipped cream to the cooled rice pudding and gently fold with a rubber spatula until the whipped cream is fully incorporated and the rice pudding is airy and fluffy. Sprinkle the top with the flowers or petals and serve at room temperature. (Alternatively, if you like your rice pudding cold, refrigerate it for at least 1 hour before topping with the flowers or petals.) The rice pudding (without flowers) keeps in an airtight container in the refrigerator for up to 3 days. Stir before serving.

EARL GREY BUCKWHEAT PANCAKE TOWER

SERVES 8

I know, you were probably expecting a crepe recipe, but I've always had a soft spot for pancakes. There's something so wonderfully satisfying about a towering stack of them, all warm and golden. One afternoon, at my friend Molly's place in Brooklyn, I thought, why not turn pancakes into more of a showstopper? And so, this layered pancake cake was born.

The buckwheat and Earl Grey lend a lovely earthiness to the pancakes, which are a bit more old-fashioned in style. To get that dramatic, tiered effect, use a wide pan so you can make pancakes in a variety of sizes. If you're feeling a bit less ambitious, make them all the same size and serve them simply, with the whipped cream, jam, fruit, and maple syrup on the side. Either way, make them for someone you love. Or someone you hate—I promise they'll love you afterward.

EARL GREY PANCAKES

3½ cups / 840ml whole milk
6 tablespoons loose Earl Grey tea leaves
Juice of 1 lemon
2 cups / 280g buckwheat flour
2 cups / 280g all-purpose flour
⅔ cup / 130g sugar
2 teaspoons cornstarch
2 teaspoons baking soda
2 teaspoons baking powder
½ teaspoon grated orange zest (from 1 medium orange)
1 teaspoon fine sea salt
1 stick / 113g unsalted butter, cut into small pieces, plus more for cooking the pancakes
4 large eggs
2 teaspoons vanilla extract

PANCAKE TOWER

12 cups / 1,200g Vanilla Bean Whipped Cream (page 221)
About 1½ cups / 450g blackberry jam, homemade (recipe follows) or store-bought
Fresh blackberries and raspberries
Maple syrup
Small edible flowers (see page 88), for decorating

1. FOR THE EARL GREY PANCAKES: In a medium saucepan, warm the milk over low heat just until steam starts to rise from the surface; do not let it come to a simmer or boil. Remove from the heat, stir in the Earl Grey tea leaves, cover, and let stand for 30 minutes.

2. Pour through a fine-mesh sieve set over a medium bowl, pressing on the tea to extract as much flavor as possible (discard the tea leaves). Let the milk cool completely.

3. Add the lemon juice to the cooled infused milk and let stand for a few minutes to create a "buttermilk."

4. In a large bowl, whisk together the flours, sugar, cornstarch, baking soda, baking powder, orange zest, and salt.

5. In a small saucepan, melt the butter over medium-low heat. Remove from the heat.

6. Create a hole in the middle of the flour mixture, then add the eggs, vanilla, melted butter, and the infused "buttermilk" and whisk until there are no large clumps. Let the batter stand at room temperature for 30 minutes, which will give the pancakes more rise.

7. In a wide, preferably nonstick, skillet, melt some butter over medium-low heat. Pour about 1 cup / 240ml of batter into the pan, creating an 8-inch / 20cm or wider pancake—the batter is thick so you may need to spread it a bit. Cook the pancake, without moving it, until the bubbles on top start to pop, 1 to 2 minutes. Flip the pancake and cook until the other side is golden, 1 to 2 more minutes. Transfer it to a plate and cover with aluminum foil to keep warm. Repeat to cook more pancakes, making each pancake about ½ inch / 13mm smaller than the previous one, until you make a 1-inch / 2.5cm pancake for the top of the tower. Add more butter to the pan as you cook and adjust the heat as needed; the

RECIPE CONTINUES

pancakes may cook a bit faster as they get smaller and as the pan gets hotter.

8. **FOR THE PANCAKE TOWER:** The pancakes should be warm but not so hot that the whipped cream immediately melts. Place the largest pancake on a plate that is slightly larger than it. Dollop some of the whipped cream, jam, and fresh fruit on top. Drizzle with maple syrup and place the next largest pancake on top. Repeat with the remaining pancakes, whipped cream, jam, fruit, and maple syrup to create the tower.

9. Decorate with flowers or petals (see Tips for Working with Flowers, page 85).

Blackberry Jam

MAKES 4 CUPS / 1.12KG

3 pounds / 1.4kg blackberries, fresh or thawed frozen (about 11½ cups)
4 cups / 800g sugar
1 teaspoon fine salt
Juice of 2 lemons

1. Put two small plates in the freezer.

2. In a large Dutch oven or heavy-bottomed saucepan, combine the blackberries and sugar and cook over medium-high heat, stirring frequently to keep the fruit from burning. Using a large stainless steel spoon, skim off the reddish purple foam that rises to the top as the mixture comes to a boil.

3. When the jam starts to feel a bit thick, scoop a spoonful onto one of the frozen plates and wait 1 to 2 minutes for it to come to room temperature. Tip the plate from side to side. If the jam is ready, it will hold its shape on the plate rather than run down it. If you're not sure, try running a spoon through the jam on the plate—if it holds the line, it's ready. The jam should have a smooth texture studded with blackberry seeds but no chunks of fruit. If needed, continue cooking the jam until it sets on the second frozen plate.

4. Once the jam passes the plate test, add the salt and lemon juice, then remove it from the heat. If you want to seal the jam in jars for longer term storage, do so while it's still hot (see How to Can Jams and Curds, page 187).

5. Otherwise, let the jam stand in the pot, without stirring, to cool and thicken for about 30 minutes, then transfer it to jars or airtight containers but do not cover. Let the jam cool to room temperature, then cover and refrigerate for up to 2 weeks. You can cool the jam in the refrigerator, but it's important to allow the jam to fully cool before covering, as condensation could drip back into your beautiful work and loosen the texture.

DE LAMARTINE
MADAME DE GIRARDIN
ŒUVRES COMPLÈTES

How to
CAN JAMS AND CURDS

Canning is one of the best ways to enjoy the rich flavor of cherry jam in winter or tangy lemon curd in summer. I grew up on a farm in France, where we harvested more fruits and vegetables than our family could eat, and tradition dictated that food you preserved could last you through winter, when very little food is coming out of the ground. This meant canning was a regular activity throughout my childhood. I grew up using a quicker, more home-style approach that my mum taught me, which I'll share later, but first, here's a step-by-step guide to the proper way. If you're making jams and curds to use in cakes, there's no need to seal them in jars, as they'll keep in airtight containers in the refrigerator (two weeks for jams and one week for curds). But once you realize how easy it is to make homemade jams and curds—and how delicious the results—you'll likely want to do it more often and start preserving them. Both make lovely gifts.

1. Begin by sterilizing the glass jars: Place the jars on a baking sheet and put them in a 300°F / 150°C oven for at least 20 minutes. You can reuse jars, but make sure they don't have any cracks.

2. Put the lids and rings in a heatproof bowl, then cover with boiling water and let stand until ready to use. Always use new lids and rings each time.

3. Fill a large, tall stockpot with enough water to cover the jars, then place it over high heat, cover, and bring to a boil. This is your hot water bath.

4. Wearing oven gloves, carefully remove the sterilized jars from the oven. Using a funnel, spoon, or ladle, place the hot jam or curd, just out of the pot, into the sterilized jars, leaving about ¼ inch / 6mm of headspace, so there's room for the jam to expand.

5. Dip a clean kitchen towel in hot water and wipe the jars clean. Remove the lids and rings from the hot water and use a clean kitchen towel to dry them completely. Screw on the lids, but don't seal them too tight.

6. Using a jar lifter, carefully lower the jars into the hot water bath and boil them for 15 minutes. You'll see some air bubbles coming out of the jars, but that will subside as the jars are sealed. If the water boils down, add more boiling water to make sure the jars are always fully covered. The jars may rattle a bit.

7. Carefully remove the jars from the hot water, then place them on a clean dry kitchen towel. Test for the "pop" in the lids by pressing your finger in the center of each. If there is still air inside the jar, the lid will press down, but if the jars are fully sealed, they won't move. If any jars are not sealed, curd will still keep in the refrigerator for up to 1 week and jam will keep for up to 2 weeks.

8. Let the jars sit at room temperature until completely cool. Once the jars are completely cool, you can remove the rings. I also like to cut rounds of fabric and secure them to the tops of the jars with ribbon or rubber bands. Store in a cool, dry place for up to 1 year.

ALTERNATIVE HOME-STYLE APPROACH

My family's way of canning is a touch more homemade. Start by sterilizing the jars in a 350°F / 180°C oven for 20 minutes and covering the lids and rings with boiling water. You can leave the jars in the oven until you're ready to use them but drain the lids and rings and dry them completely with a clean kitchen towel before using. Wearing oven gloves and using a funnel, ladle the hot jam or curd—just out of the pot—into the jars, then dip a kitchen towel in hot water and quickly wipe the jars clean. Next, add the lids and rings and firmly tighten. Flip the jars over and let them stand, upside down, for 45 minutes. You should end up with lids that don't pop or don't move up and down—that means you have sealed jam or curd.

SAGE SEA SALT BROWNIES

MAKES ABOUT 12 BROWNIES

These brownies are a twist on the classic, and if you chill them overnight, the sage notes deepen, making them even more delicious the next day. A sprinkle of Maldon sea salt on top enhances the flavors, while a few decorative sage leaves add an elegant touch. Adjust the baking time to suit your personal preferences: If you like softer, fudgier brownies, bake them for 20 minutes, but if you prefer firmer brownies, aim for closer to 25 minutes. Give the brownies time to cool completely, so they have the perfect texture—and are easier to cut!

2 sticks / 226g unsalted butter
10 large fresh sage leaves, roughly chopped, plus more leaves for decorating
Softened unsalted butter, for the baking pan
3¼ ounces / 90g dark chocolate, chopped
1 cup / 80g unsweetened Dutch-process cocoa powder
½ cup / 70g all-purpose flour
½ teaspoon fine sea salt
1¼ cups plus 2 tablespoons / 275g sugar
3 large eggs, at room temperature
⅓ cup / 45g roughly chopped raw almonds
¼ teaspoon Maldon sea salt

1. In a small saucepan, melt the butter over medium-low heat. Remove from the heat, then stir in the chopped sage, cover, and let stand for 30 minutes.

2. Set a rack in the middle of the oven and preheat to 350°F / 180°C. Lightly butter the bottom and sides of an 8-inch / 20cm square metal baking pan, then line the pan with parchment paper, leaving about 1 inch / 2.5cm hanging over the sides.

3. Fill a medium saucepan with about 1 inch / 2.5cm of water and bring to a simmer over medium-low heat. Add the dark chocolate to a large heatproof bowl, then set the bowl over the pan of simmering water, making sure the water does not touch the bottom of the bowl. Warm the chocolate, stirring occasionally, until melted. Remove the bowl from the pan (careful—it will be warm!) and use a clean kitchen towel to carefully wipe any condensation from the bottom of the bowl.

4. Pour the sage-infused butter through a fine-mesh sieve set over the bowl of melted chocolate, pressing on the sage to extract as much flavor as possible (discard the sage). Stir until the butter is fully incorporated into the melted chocolate.

5. Sift the cocoa powder and flour into a medium bowl. Add the salt.

6. In a stand mixer fitted with the whisk, whip the sugar and eggs on high speed until fluffy and doubled in volume, 2 to 3 minutes. Add the chocolate mixture and whip on medium-low speed, scraping the bottom and sides of the bowl as needed, until incorporated, about 30 seconds. Gradually add the flour mixture and mix on low speed, scraping the bowl as needed, until just combined, about 30 seconds. Do not overmix, as you don't want to lose all the fluffy texture you created by whipping the eggs and sugar.

7. Remove the bowl from the stand mixer, then scrape it. Add the almonds and gently fold with a rubber spatula until incorporated.

8. Pour the mixture into the prepared pan, smoothing the top. Sprinkle with the Maldon salt and a few sage leaves for decoration.

9. Bake until slightly cracked and firm along the edges but soft and gooey in the middle, 20 to 25 minutes.

10. Let the brownies cool completely in the pan on a wire rack. Carefully wiggle the parchment paper to release the brownies from the pan, then lift the parchment and use it to place the brownies on a cutting board. Cut into equal squares for serving. The brownies keep in an airtight container in the refrigerator for up to 5 days, or can be well wrapped and frozen for up to 2 months.

BLACKBERRY VIOLET ÉCLAIR CAKE

SERVES 8

Every Saturday, after ballet class, my mum would pick me up, and we'd stop at the local patisserie for an éclair. It wasn't the healthiest treat, but it always made me happy—and definitely kept me from complaining about going to ballet! To turn that post-ballet comfort into a dessert for a crowd, I created this flower-shaped éclair cake. It's perfect for sharing and makes for an impressive and playful centerpiece. I chose the flavor of the cake because of my time studying in Toulouse, a city renowned for using violets in food. For the pastry cream filling, I've swapped out the milk for blackberry syrup, which adds deep flavor and vibrant color. You can add unsweetened Dutch-process cocoa powder to the éclair dough (add ¼ cup / 20g to the flour) for an even more dramatic look.

BLACKBERRY VIOLET PASTRY CREAM

17 ounces / 510g blackberries, fresh or thawed frozen (about 4¼ cups)
1 cup / 200g granulated sugar
Juice of ½ lemon
4 large eggs yolks
½ cup plus 1 tablespoon / 70g cornstarch
2 teaspoons violet syrup
½ teaspoon vanilla extract
¼ teaspoon fine sea salt
3 tablespoons unsalted butter, cut into small pieces

ÉCLAIR DOUGH

½ cup plus 2 teaspoons / 130ml whole milk
7 tablespoons / 105g unsalted butter, cut into small pieces
1 tablespoon granulated sugar
¼ teaspoon fine sea salt
1 cup plus 2 tablespoons / 150g all-purpose flour
5 large eggs, at room temperature

BLACKBERRY VIOLET GLAZE

½ cup / 60g blackberries, fresh or thawed frozen
1 tablespoon freshly squeezed lemon juice (from 1 medium lemon)
1 teaspoon violet syrup
3 tablespoons unsalted butter, melted
2 tablespoons heavy cream, at room temperature
1½ cups / 180g powdered sugar, sifted

1. FOR THE BLACKBERRY VIOLET PASTRY CREAM: In a deep medium saucepan set over medium heat, combine the blackberries, ¼ cup / 50g of the granulated sugar, the lemon juice, and ¼ cup / 60ml water. Using an immersion blender, blend on low speed until it looks like a puree, about 2 minutes. Remove the blender and bring the mixture to a boil over medium heat, while stirring occasionally with a wooden spoon. Continue boiling and stirring for 3 minutes.

2. Remove from the heat, then pour through a fine-mesh sieve set over a medium bowl, pressing on the fruit to extract as much juice as possible (discard the skins and seeds). Clean the saucepan, then return the strained mixture to it, and bring to a simmer over low heat.

3. Meanwhile, in a medium bowl, whisk together the egg yolks, the remaining ¾ cup / 150g of granulated sugar, the cornstarch, violet syrup, vanilla, and salt until fully combined. It will be a thick paste.

4. Once the blackberry mixture is simmering, remove from the heat. While whisking constantly, gradually add the blackberry mixture to the egg yolk mixture in three batches, whisking until smooth, thick, and dark red. Pour this into the saucepan, set over medium-high heat, and cook, whisking constantly and scraping the edges and corners of the pan to prevent burning, until thick bubbles form and it has the consistency of pastry cream, about 5 minutes. Continue cooking and whisking for 30 seconds more, then remove from the heat and gradually add the butter, one piece at a time, whisking until melted and fully incorporated. Transfer the pastry cream to a large bowl and cover with plastic wrap, pressing the plastic wrap directly onto the surface of the pastry cream to prevent a skin from forming. Refrigerate until cold, about 2 hours.

5. FOR THE ÉCLAIR DOUGH: Set a rack in the middle of the oven and preheat to 475°F / 250°C. Line the bottom of a 13 × 18-inch / 33 × 45cm or similarly sized

RECIPE CONTINUES

baking sheet with parchment paper. Use a pen or marker to draw the outline of a large flower in the middle of the baking sheet. The flower should measure about 11 × 11 inches / 28 × 28cm from outside the petals and there should be a space in the middle that measures about 3 inches / 7.5cm. Draw a ring, roughly 2 inches / 5cm in diameter, in the middle to create the center of the flower. Flip the parchment over so this guide is on the bottom.

6. In a medium saucepan, combine the milk, butter, granulated sugar, salt, and ½ cup / 120ml water. Warm the mixture over medium heat, whisking occasionally, until the milk is simmering, and the butter is melted. Remove from the heat, then add the flour all at once and stir with a rubber spatula until the mixture comes together into a smooth, wet dough, about 1 minute. Set the saucepan over medium heat and cook, stirring vigorously and pushing the dough around with the spatula to dry it out, until the dough leaves the sides of the pan and forms a stiff ball, about 2 minutes.

7. Transfer the dough to a stand mixer fitted with the paddle and beat on medium speed for about 30 seconds to cool it down. Add the eggs, one at a time, and beat, scraping down the bottom and sides of the bowl before each addition and again at the end, for about 30 seconds per egg. The dough may appear curdled when adding the eggs, but don't panic—it will come back together once it's fully mixed. Continue beating until the dough is shiny, thick, and smooth, about 30 seconds. Remove the paddle attachment from the stand mixer and use it to scoop up some of the dough, letting it fall back into the bowl. It should form a triangle or "V" shape when it's ready.

8. Transfer the dough to a piping bag fitted with a plain round tip with a ½-inch / 13mm or similar diameter. Holding the piping bag at a 45-degree angle to the lined baking sheet and applying even pressure, pipe a thick line along the guide you drew on the parchment to create the outline of a flower. Repeat to pipe a second thick line just inside the outline of the flower. Repeat again to pipe a third thick line on top of and in between the first two lines. Using your guide, pipe a large dollop in the middle to create the center of the flower.

9. Turn off the oven, then place the baking sheet inside and let set for 10 minutes. Without opening the oven door, turn the oven to 325°F / 160°C and bake until the cake is golden brown and there are no tiny wet bubbles on the surface, 50 to 55 minutes.

10. Set the baking sheet on a wire rack and let the cake cool completely.

11. Remove the violet blackberry pastry cream from the refrigerator and transfer it to a medium bowl. Whisk it briefly to bring back its creamy texture, then transfer to a piping bag fitted with a small round tip.

12. Carefully flip the cooled éclair cake upside down on the baking sheet. Use a slightly larger open star pastry tip to poke holes, about 1½ inches / 4cm apart, in the bottom of the éclair cake (both the "petals" and center), making sure not to break through the top of the cake.

13. Holding the piping bag in your dominant hand, gently press the pastry tip into one of the holes in the bottom of the éclair cake, then gently squeeze the piping bag to fill the éclair cake—it will expand slightly when it's full. Repeat to fill the remaining holes, then wipe off any excess filling.

14. FOR THE BLACKBERRY VIOLET GLAZE: In a blender, combine the blackberries, lemon juice, and violet syrup and blend until the fruit breaks down and the mixture has a sauce-like consistency. Pour through a fine-mesh sieve set over a small bowl (discard the skins and seeds).

15. In a stand mixer fitted with the whisk, whip the melted butter and heavy cream on medium speed for 30 seconds. Add the powdered sugar in two batches and whip, scraping the bowl as needed, until fully combined, about 30 seconds per batch. Scrape the bowl, then add 2 tablespoons of the violet blackberry mixture and whip on high speed until fully incorporated, about 30 seconds. The glaze should be a dark reddish-purple color. Scrape the bowl, then add 1 more tablespoon of the violet blackberry mixture and whip for 30 seconds. The glaze should have an even color and be thick but spreadable—the consistency should be similar to royal icing. If the glaze is too stiff, gradually add 1 more tablespoon of

the violet blackberry mixture, and whip for 30 seconds more. Press plastic wrap directly onto the surface to prevent a skin from forming and refrigerate until ready to use; you may need to whip it to bring back the desired consistency. The glaze can be made up to 3 days ahead and kept in the refrigerator.

16. Carefully pour the violet blackberry glaze onto a 13 × 18-inch / 33 × 45cm or similarly sized baking sheet and use a small offset spatula to gently spread the glaze until it covers an area as large as the flower part of the éclair cake. Gently hold the flower, with the holes facing up, over the glaze, then carefully lower it into the glaze, pressing gently on the edges to make sure the glaze covers the entire top surface. Wiggle the cake slightly to release it from the glaze, then carefully flip it back over and set it on a large plate or platter for serving. If there are any gaps in the glaze, use a spoon or small offset spatula to fill them in. If the glaze doesn't look smooth in some spots, dip a spoon in boiling water, then dry it and carefully run the back over the glaze to smooth it out. Repeat this process with the center of the flower and arrange it in the middle of the plate or platter.

17. Set the éclair cake, glaze-side up, in the refrigerator to firm up the glaze for 1 to 2 hours. Remove from the fridge about 30 minutes before serving.

GOÛTER

The French Tradition of a 4 p.m. Treat

AZAY-LE-RIDEAU

TAHINI BLACK SESAME EARL GREY MARBLE LOAF

MAKES ONE 9 × 5 × 3-INCH / 23 × 13 × 7.5CM LOAF

I try to avoid generalizations, but I promise you that almost any French person will tell you they grew up eating marble loaf. With its signature swirls, this cake is a beloved part of daily life—whether it's for breakfast, an after-school goûter, or even a birthday cake. While there are already countless classic recipes out there, I've given my version a twist by adding creamy tahini, aromatic Earl Grey tea, and nutty, rich black sesame.

MARBLE LOAF

- Canola oil spray or canola oil, for the pan
- 1¼ cups / 175g all-purpose flour
- 1¾ teaspoons baking powder
- ½ teaspoon baking soda
- 1½ teaspoons fine sea salt
- ½ cup plus 2 tablespoons / 150g whole-milk yogurt (not Greek), at room temperature
- ½ cup plus 2 tablespoons / 135g well-mixed tahini, at room temperature
- 1 cup / 200g granulated sugar
- 2 large eggs, at room temperature
- 1 teaspoon vanilla extract
- ¼ teaspoon grated orange zest (from 1 medium orange)
- ¾ cup / 180ml canola oil
- 6 tablespoons / 25g loose Earl Grey tea leaves, finely ground
- 3 tablespoons black sesame seeds, finely ground

EARL GREY MILK

- ¼ cup / 60ml whole milk
- 1 tablespoon loose Earl Grey tea leaves

EARL GREY GLAZE

- 1½ cups plus 3 tablespoons / 200g powdered sugar, sifted, plus more as needed
- 1 teaspoon loose Earl Grey tea leaves, finely ground
- ¼ teaspoon fine sea salt
- ⅛ teaspoon grated orange zest (from 1 medium orange)
- Earl Grey tea leaves and small edible flowers (see page 88), for decorating

1. **FOR THE MARBLE LOAF:** Set a rack in the middle of the oven and preheat to 300°F / 150°C. Spray or brush a 9 × 5 × 3-inch / 23 × 13 × 7.5cm loaf pan with canola oil, then line the pan with parchment paper, leaving about 1 inch / 2.5cm hanging over the sides.

2. Sift the flour, baking powder, and baking soda into a medium bowl. Add the salt.

3. In a small bowl, whisk together the yogurt and tahini.

4. In a stand mixer fitted with the paddle, beat the granulated sugar, eggs, vanilla, and orange zest on medium-high speed until pale and thick, about 3 minutes. Scrape down the bottom and sides of the bowl. On medium speed, slowly add the canola oil. Once all the oil is added, scrape the bowl, then beat on medium-high speed for about 1 minute to fully emulsify.

5. On low speed, add the flour mixture in three batches, alternating with the yogurt mixture in two batches and scraping the bowl before each addition. Mix just until there are no streaks. Do not overmix!

6. Remove half of the batter from the stand mixer and set it aside.

7. Add the ground Earl Grey tea and the ground black sesame seeds to the batter in the stand mixer and beat on medium speed, scraping the bowl as needed, just until incorporated, about 1 minute. Scrape the bowl.

8. Dollop or pipe a few large scoops of each batter into the prepared pan, alternating between the two batters. To create a dramatic swirl, insert a long skewer or a long, thin knife into the batter, making sure the tip reaches the bottom of the pan. Drag it through the batter in a single long figure-eight motion two or three times, but do not swirl it too much or you won't get the marble effect. Gently tap the pan on the countertop to ensure there are no air pockets between the two batters. Bake until a skewer inserted in the center of the loaf comes out clean, 50 to 55 minutes.

RECIPE CONTINUES

9. Set the pan on a wire rack set inside a baking sheet and let the loaf cool for 30 minutes. Carefully wiggle the parchment paper to release the loaf from the pan, then lift the parchment and use it to place the loaf directly on the rack. Let cool completely.

10. FOR THE EARL GREY MILK: In a small saucepan, warm the milk over low heat just until steam starts to rise from the surface; do not let it come to a simmer or bubble. Remove from the heat, then stir in the whole Earl Grey tea leaves, cover, and let stand for 30 minutes.

11. Pour through a fine-mesh sieve set over a small bowl, pressing on the tea to extract as much flavor as possible (discard the tea leaves). Let the milk cool completely.

12. FOR THE EARL GREY GLAZE: In a stand mixer fitted with the whisk, mix the powdered sugar, 3 tablespoons of the cooled Earl Grey milk, the ground Earl Grey tea, salt, and orange zest and whip on low speed for 30 seconds. Increase the speed to medium and whip until fully combined, thick, and opaque—it should be the consistency of royal icing—about 30 seconds. If the glaze seems too runny, let it stand for a few minutes to firm up. If it's still runny, gradually add more powdered sugar, 1 tablespoon at a time, until you achieve the desired consistency. The glaze should be quite thick, but if it's too stiff to spread on the cake, gradually drizzle in more of the Earl Grey milk.

13. With the loaf still on the wire rack set inside the baking sheet, slowly pour the glaze over the cooled loaf, pushing it to completely cover the top and slightly drip down the sides. Before the glaze sets, sprinkle the top with Earl Grey tea leaves, then press the flowers (see Tips for Working with Flowers, page 85) into the loaf. Enjoy right away. The loaf (without flowers) keeps in an airtight container at room temperature for up to 3 days.

SALTED DARK CHOCOLATE CHIP COOKIES

MAKES 20 TO 24 COOKIES

Many children grow up loving their mother's homemade chocolate chip cookies, but not me. It took me two and a half years to perfect my recipe, but these are now a From Lucie favorite and have even been called one of the city's best cookies by the *New York Times*.

There are several secrets behind my ultimate chocolate chip cookie. Using the best chocolate is obviously key, but my recipe uses a combination of dark and milk chocolate fèves (the large oval-shaped chocolate discs used by pastry chefs), which create pools of shiny, gooey chocolate that are both beautiful and irresistible. That being said, large or small chocolate chips (or even chopped chocolate) also work. Instead of creaming the butter and sugar as for most chocolate chip cookie recipes, I melt the butter to give the cookies their signature crunchy exterior and gooey interior. Note that this does make the dough a bit softer than you may be used to. Lastly, I refrigerate the dough for an hour, shape it into balls, and then freeze the balls for at least 30 minutes before baking. The time in the fridge gives the cookies a nuttiness, while freezing helps maintain their round shape and wonderfully soft texture.

My mum hasn't tried these yet, but hopefully she'll like mine more than I like hers!

3 sticks / 339g unsalted butter
3¼ cups / 455g all-purpose flour
¾ teaspoon baking soda
1½ teaspoons fine sea salt
1½ cups / 300g granulated sugar
2¼ cups / 450g (packed) light brown sugar
3 large eggs, at room temperature
1 tablespoon vanilla extract
11¼ ounces / 320g dark chocolate fèves or large chips, preferably 64% to 72% cacao
3¾ ounces / 105g milk chocolate fèves or large chips
Maldon sea salt, for sprinkling

1. In a medium saucepan, melt the butter over medium-low heat. Remove from the heat and let cool slightly.

2. Sift the flour and baking soda into a medium bowl. Add the fine salt.

3. In a stand mixer fitted with the paddle, mix both sugars on low speed for about 30 seconds. Add the melted butter and beat on medium-low speed until silky and sticky, about 30 seconds. Add the eggs, one at a time, and beat on medium speed, scraping down the bottom and sides of the bowl before each addition and again at the end, until fully incorporated. Add the vanilla and beat, scraping the bowl as needed, until pale and fluffy, about 3 minutes.

4. Add the flour mixture in three batches and mix on low speed, scraping the bowl before each addition, just until there are no streaks. Do not overmix! Add both chocolates and mix until just incorporated.

5. Remove the bowl from the stand mixer and place a piece of plastic wrap directly on the surface of the dough, then refrigerate for about 1 hour.

6. Line a pan or a flat-bottomed container that fits in your freezer with parchment paper. Using a large ice cream scoop with a 2-inch / 5cm or similar diameter, scoop the dough into large balls and place the balls, in a single layer, on the lined pan. Wrap the pan or container in plastic wrap and freeze for 30 minutes to 1 hour before baking. (Once the balls are frozen, they can be stored in a zip-top freezer bag and kept in the freezer for up to 1 month; bake straight from frozen.)

7. When ready to bake, set a rack in the middle of the oven and preheat to 350°F / 180°C. Line the bottom of a 13 × 18-inch / 33 × 45cm or similarly sized baking sheet with a silicone baking mat or parchment paper.

RECIPE CONTINUES

8. Arrange 3 balls of frozen dough on the prepared pan, allowing plenty of room for spreading, then sprinkle generously with the Maldon salt. Bake for about 8 minutes, then quickly rotate the pan and bake until the cookies are crunchy around the edges but still soft in the middle, about 8 minutes more.

9. Let the cookies cool on the baking sheet on a wire rack for about 15 minutes. Use a metal spatula to transfer the cookies to the rack. Enjoy right away or let cool completely. Repeat to bake as many cookies as you like. The cookies keep in an airtight container at room temperature for up to 3 days, or can be well wrapped and frozen for up to 2 months.

CANELÉS

MAKES ABOUT 16 CANELÉS

Coming from Bordeaux, where canelés were invented, I've had my share of incredible and not so good canelés. Over the years, I've learned that I love them most when baked in traditional copper molds. Copper is a highly conductive material, which helps distribute the heat evenly throughout the molds, resulting in canelés that are perfectly caramelized on the outside with soft custard-like interiors and plenty of air pockets. The next best option is to use a non-copper metal mold. You can use silicone, but the canelés will be paler in color with a softer, spongier texture. They will still be fantastic! You can also use slightly smaller molds—just keep an eye on them, as they may not need as much time in the oven.

Canelés are traditionally flavored with rum, but my mother's friend Catherine, from her sewing group growing up, always used half rum and half pastis, an anise-flavored spirit from the South of France. I find them so much more delicious this way. These are a bite-size treat perfect with an espresso after a long lunch.

4 cups / 960ml whole milk
1 vanilla bean
2½ cups / 500g sugar
1½ cups / 210g all-purpose flour
2 large eggs, at room temperature
6 large egg yolks, at room temperature
½ cup / 120ml dark rum
½ cup / 120ml pastis, preferably Ricard
½ teaspoon lemon extract
½ teaspoon orange extract
½ teaspoon almond extract
Softened unsalted butter, for the molds

1. Put the milk in a medium saucepan. Split the vanilla bean in half lengthwise, then scrape the seeds into the milk, add the pod, and bring to a boil over medium-low heat.

2. Meanwhile, in a large bowl, whisk together the sugar, flour, whole eggs, and egg yolks until fully combined into a very thick paste.

3. Once the milk is boiling, turn off the heat and carefully remove the vanilla pod. While whisking, gradually add the milk to the sugar mixture. Continue whisking until the milk is fully incorporated and the mixture is uniform. Add the rum and pastis, along with the lemon, orange, and almond extracts, and whisk until the mixture is completely smooth, with no lumps, about 30 seconds. It should have a very thin consistency. Cover and refrigerate for 24 hours.

4. When ready to bake the canelés, set a rack in the lower third of the oven and preheat to 425°F / 220°C. Use a pastry brush to very generously brush butter on the insides of 12 metal canelé molds (or a 12-cavity metal canelé mold). Place the molds on a baking sheet for baking.

5. Pour the batter into the canelé molds; refrigerate any leftover batter. Bake until the canelés are dark brown on the outside and yellow in the center, about 1 hour 10 minutes—the outsides should be slightly firm, and the insides should be soft.

6. Carefully turn them out onto the rack and let cool completely. If the canelés don't slip out easily, knock the molds on the countertop to loosen them. Repeat with the remaining batter to make more canelés.

7. Serve the canelés as is. Canelés are best within a few hours of baking, but they keep in an airtight container at room temperature for up to 3 days. Reheat in a 450°F / 230°C oven for 5 minutes. Let cool until the exteriors harden. The canelés can also be wrapped individually in plastic wrap and frozen for up to 1 month. Remove the plastic wrap and place directly from frozen in a 500°F / 260°C oven for 5 minutes. Set on a wire rack to cool for 30 minutes, but leave the oven on. Return the canelés to the oven for 5 more minutes, then let cool until the exteriors harden.

LEMON THYME BARS

MAKES TWELVE 1½ × 4-INCH / 4 × 10CM BARS

These bars are a true lemon person's dream and offer a fragrant blend of citrus and fresh herbs. The lemon curd thickens quickly, so keep a close eye on it and stir constantly to prevent it from overcooking. The shortbread crust is easy to make, and I use a metal baking pan to ensure even baking. Lightly greasing the pan helps the parchment paper stick and makes it easier to press the dough into the pan. Chilling the bars allows the flavors to meld together beautifully and I personally prefer to serve them cold. Last but not least, I love topping these with edible buds for a delicate finishing touch.

SHORTBREAD

Softened unsalted butter, for the pan
½ cup / 100g sugar
1 tablespoon fresh thyme leaves, roughly chopped
2 cups / 280g all-purpose flour
½ teaspoon fine sea salt
2 sticks / 226g unsalted butter, melted and cooled
2 teaspoons vanilla extract

LEMON CURD

4 large eggs, at room temperature
6 large egg yolks, at room temperature
½ cup / 100g sugar
⅓ cup / 45g all-purpose flour
2 teaspoons fresh thyme leaves, roughly chopped
1¼ cups / 300ml freshly squeezed lemon juice (from about 7 medium lemons)
2 teaspoons grated lemon zest (from 1 medium lemon)
Small edible flowers (see page 88), for decorating

1. FOR THE SHORTBREAD: Set a rack in the middle of the oven and preheat to 350°F / 180°C. Lightly butter the bottom and sides of an 8-inch / 20cm square metal baking pan, then line the pan with parchment paper, leaving about 1 inch / 2.5cm hanging over the sides.

2. In the bowl of a stand mixer, combine the sugar and thyme and use your fingers to massage the mixture, releasing the herb's oils. Sift the flour into the bowl, then add the salt. Using the paddle, mix on low speed for about 15 seconds to incorporate the flour. Gradually add the melted butter and the vanilla and mix for 30 seconds. Increase the speed to medium and beat until the butter is fully incorporated and the dough is smooth and sticky, about 1 minute.

3. Using your hands, press the dough into the prepared pan, spreading it into the corners and creating an even layer. Bake for 12 minutes, then quickly rotate the pan and continue baking until evenly golden, about 12 minutes more.

4. Let the shortbread cool completely in the pan on a wire rack. Leave the oven on, but lower the oven temperature to 300°F / 150°C.

5. FOR THE LEMON CURD: Fill a medium saucepan with about 1 inch / 2.5cm of water and bring to a simmer over medium-low heat. In a large heatproof bowl, whisk together the whole eggs, egg yolks, sugar, flour, and thyme. Set the bowl over the pan of simmering water, making sure the water does not touch the bottom of the bowl. Add the lemon juice and cook, stirring constantly with a rubber spatula until the curd is thick, about 5 minutes. To test, dip a wooden spoon in the curd and use your finger to draw a line through the curd; if the line holds, the curd is ready.

6. Pour through a fine-mesh sieve set over a large bowl, pressing on the thyme to extract as much flavor as possible (discard the thyme). Stir in the lemon zest.

7. Pour the curd over the cooled shortbread crust, return to the oven, and bake until the curd is just set, 25 to 30 minutes.

8. Let the lemon bars cool in the pan on a wire rack for 30 minutes. Carefully wiggle the parchment paper to release the bars from the pan, then lift the parchment and use it to place the bars directly on the rack. Let cool for 30 minutes more, then refrigerate for about 1 hour.

9. Cut the lemon bars into twelve 1½ × 4-inch / 4 × 10cm rectangles. Press a flower into the end of each bar. If you prefer to serve the bars at room temperature, remove them from the refrigerator about 2 hours in advance. The bars keep in an airtight container in the refrigerator for up to 3 days, or can be well wrapped and frozen for up to 3 months.

ROSE RASPBERRY SANDWICH BISCUITS

MAKES 18 TO 20 BISCUITS

This recipe brings me back to teatime with friends and family, especially with Margaret, my best friend's grandmother, who always serves the shortbread and butter biscuits of your dreams. As you may know by now, I could put jam on just about anything, but the combination of jam and shortbread is one of my absolute favorites.

These biscuits are delicious, but they also offer a fun opportunity to get creative with design and presentation before eating them alongside your tea or coffee. You can also adjust the texture—roll the dough slightly thicker for biscuits with a soft interior and crisp exterior, or thinner for all-around crunch.

BISCUITS

1 stick plus 1 tablespoon / 128g unsalted butter, at room temperature
¾ cup / 90g powdered sugar, sifted, plus more for dusting
¼ cup / 25g almond flour
¾ teaspoon fine sea salt
1 large egg, at room temperature
1½ cups / 210g all-purpose flour
¼ cup / 4g edible rose petals (optional)

ROSE RASPBERRY JAM FILLING

¾ cup / 225 raspberry jam, homemade (page 95) or store-bought
¾ teaspoon rose water

1. FOR THE BISCUITS: In a stand mixer fitted with the paddle, beat the butter on medium speed until creamy, about 1 minute. Scrape down the bottom and sides of the bowl, then add the powdered sugar, almond flour, and salt and beat on medium-low speed, scraping the bowl as needed, until smooth and creamy, 1 to 2 minutes. Add the egg and beat on medium speed until fully incorporated, 2 to 3 minutes. Gradually add the all-purpose flour, followed by the rose petals (if using), and mix on low speed, scraping the bowl as needed, just until the dough comes together, about 1 minute total. Shape the dough into a ball and slightly flatten it, then wrap the dough in plastic wrap and refrigerate for at least 2 hours.

2. When ready to bake, set a rack in the middle of the oven and preheat to 300°F / 150°C. Line two 13 × 18-inch / 33 × 45cm or similarly sized baking sheets with silicone mats or parchment paper.

3. On a lightly floured surface, use a floured rolling pin to roll the dough until about ⅛ inch / 3mm thick. Use your favorite 2-inch / 5cm cookie cutters to cut the dough into shapes. Using matching 1¼-inch / 3cm cutters, cut a small hole in the center of half the cookies. The cookies with holes will be the tops of your sandwiches; the holes are for snacking.

4. Arrange the cookies on the prepared baking sheets, leaving space in between. Bake, one baking sheet at a time, until the edges are lightly golden, 15 to 20 minutes.

5. Let the cookies cool completely on the baking sheets on wire racks. Repeat to bake the remaining cookies.

6. FOR THE ROSE RASPBERRY JAM FILLING: In a small bowl, combine the jam and rose water and mix by hand until fully combined.

7. When the cookies are cool, dust the top cookies (the ones with the holes) with powdered sugar. Spoon about 1 teaspoon of jam in the center of each bottom cookie (the ones with no holes), spreading it slightly but leaving a border around the edge. Gently press one top cookie onto each jam-covered bottom cookie to create sandwiches. The cookies are best the day they're made, as the jam softens the biscuits over time, but they keep in an airtight container in the refrigerator for up to 3 days.

BLUEBERRY FENNEL LOAF

MAKES ONE 9 × 5 × 3-INCH / 23 × 13 × 7.5CM LOAF

This might sound strange, but I only recently discovered fennel seeds. I was immediately smitten and now throw their warm aromatic flavor at almost anything sweet or savory. With their balance of licorice and ginger notes, I find fennel seeds marry perfectly with the juicy blueberries and buttery crumb of this loaf. The recipe makes more blueberry puree than is needed for the glaze, but the extra can be mixed into buttercream for a touch of flavor and a beautiful burst of deep color.

BLUEBERRY FENNEL LOAF

Canola oil spray or canola oil, for the pan
1¾ cups / 245g all-purpose flour
2½ teaspoons baking powder
⅓ cup / 45g cornmeal
4 teaspoons ground fennel
1½ teaspoons fine sea salt
¾ cup / 150g granulated sugar
⅓ cup / 80ml canola oil
2 large eggs, at room temperature
6 tablespoons / 90ml buttermilk, at room temperature
⅔ cup plus 2 tablespoons / 190g sour cream, at room temperature
1⅓ cups / 185g fresh blueberries

BLUEBERRY GLAZE

1 cup / 140g blueberries, fresh or thawed frozen
3 cups / 360g powdered sugar, plus more as needed
3 tablespoons freshly squeezed lemon juice (from 1 medium lemon)
¼ teaspoon fine sea salt
Small edible flowers (see page 88), for decorating

1. FOR THE BLUEBERRY FENNEL LOAF: Set a rack in the middle of the oven and preheat to 350°F / 180°C. Spray or brush a 9 × 5 × 3-inch / 23 × 13 × 7.5cm loaf pan with canola oil.

2. Sift the flour and baking powder into a medium bowl. Add the cornmeal, ground fennel, and salt.

3. In a stand mixer fitted with the paddle, beat the granulated sugar and canola oil on medium speed until they're fully combined and the mixture looks like wet sand, about 30 seconds. Scrape down the bottom and sides of the bowl, then add the eggs, one at a time, and beat on medium-high speed, scraping the bowl before each addition and again at the end, until fully incorporated.

4. On medium-low speed, add the flour mixture in two batches, alternating with the buttermilk and scraping the bowl before each addition. Mix just until there are no streaks. Do not overmix! Add the sour cream and beat on medium speed just until there are no streaks, about 15 seconds.

5. Remove the bowl from the stand mixer and gently fold in the blueberries with a rubber spatula until incorporated. Scrape the batter into the prepared pan, smoothing the top. The pan will be quite full, but it won't overflow. Bake until a skewer inserted in the center comes out clean, 1 hour to 1 hour 10 minutes.

6. Set the pan on a wire rack set inside a baking sheet and let the loaf cool for 30 minutes. Run a small offset spatula between the edges of the pan and the loaf, then remove the loaf from the pan, place it on the rack, and let cool completely.

7. FOR THE BLUEBERRY GLAZE: In a blender, combine the blueberries and 2 tablespoons water and pulse until mostly smooth. There might be a few bits of skin, but you can strain them out if desired.

8. Measure out 2 tablespoons of the puree and reserve the rest for another use.

9. Sift the powdered sugar into a medium bowl. Add the 2 tablespoons blueberry puree, the lemon juice, and salt and whisk until the ingredients are fully combined

and the glaze is thick and opaque—it should be the consistency of royal icing—about 1 minute. If the glaze seems too runny, let it stand for a few minutes to firm up. If it's still runny, gradually add more powdered sugar, 1 tablespoon at a time, until you achieve the desired consistency.

10. With the loaf still on the wire rack set inside the baking sheet, slowly pour the glaze over the cooled loaf, using a small offset spatula or spoon to push the glaze to completely cover the top and drip slightly down the sides. Before the glaze sets, press the flowers into the top of the loaf. Enjoy right away. The loaf (without flowers) keeps in an airtight container at room temperature for up to 3 days.

2024

SCONES

MAKES ABOUT 12 SCONES

If you asked me when I was ten years old what my favorite goûter was, besides a baguette stuffed with milk chocolate, I would've said my mother's scones. Unlike British scones, which are usually large and made with butter, my mother makes smaller scones and uses fizzy lemonade, so they are light and fluffy, while still having that perfect crumb. This means that instead of eating one and feeling a little stuffed, you can eat three or four—and then feel stuffed. At the bakery, we add some raisins for extra taste and texture, but you can skip the fruit, add a good dollop of salted butter and the jam of your choice, and call it a day. It's very important to use a really fizzy and sweet lemonade here—7UP also works!

2 cups / 280g all-purpose flour
¼ cup / 50g sugar
2½ teaspoons baking powder
⅛ teaspoon fine sea salt
⅓ cup / 45g raisins (optional)
½ cup / 120ml heavy cream
½ cup / 120ml sparkling lemonade
2 tablespoons whole milk
Salted butter and jam, for serving

1. Set a rack in the middle of the oven and preheat to 400°F / 200°C. Line one 13 × 18-inch / 33 × 45cm or similarly sized baking sheet with parchment paper.

2. Sift the flour into a medium bowl, then add the sugar, baking powder, and salt and whisk to combine. Stir in the raisins (if using). Gradually add the heavy cream, followed by the fizzy lemonade, using a fork to gently incorporate them and create a slightly sticky dough. Do not overmix!

3. Tip the dough onto a floured surface and knead about three times to bring it together without making it dense. Using a floured rolling pin or your hands, gently roll or pat the dough into a rectangle roughly 1½ inches / 4cm thick. Dip a 2-inch / 5cm round metal pastry cutter in flour, then press it firmly into the dough and quickly pull it straight upward. Repeat to cut as many scones as possible, then gently roll or pat the remaining dough into a rectangle roughly 1½ inches / 4cm thick and cut more scones. You should have about 12 scones.

4. Arrange the scones on the prepared baking sheet and brush the tops with the milk. Bake until golden on top, 12 to 15 minutes.

5. Let the scones cool briefly on the baking sheet on a wire rack. Serve with salted butter and jam. The scones are best the day they're baked but can be well wrapped and frozen for up to 2 weeks. Thaw the scones at room temperature for about 2 hours. Reheat in a 350°F / 180°C oven until warm.

ORANGE BLOSSOM MADELEINES

MAKES 18 TO 20 MADELEINES

My grandmother, a Le Cordon Bleu graduate, baked madeleines that were nothing short of perfection: tender, airy, and with a flawless hump and a delicate touch of orange blossom. While madeleines can be flavored with lemon zest, orange zest, or even more adventurous twists, there's one thing I believe is nonnegotiable: that iconic hump. Most madeleines I've seen in the US tend to lack this feature and are often glazed for decoration. While they have their charms, nothing beats pulling madeleines fresh from the oven, still warm and fragrant, their domes standing proudly. The secret to achieving that signature hump is chilling the batter, ideally overnight, before baking. The contrast between the cold batter and the hot oven creates a burst of steam, which lifts the batter into its classic shape. It's a simple trick, but one that makes all the difference—and one that will forever remind me of my granny's kitchen.

1 cup / 140g all-purpose flour
1 teaspoon baking powder
2 large eggs, at room temperature
½ cup / 100g sugar
2 teaspoons honey
⅛ teaspoon fine sea salt
1 stick plus 3 tablespoons / 143g unsalted butter, melted and cooled
2 tablespoons orange blossom water
Softened unsalted butter and flour, for the pans

1. Sift the flour and baking powder into a small bowl.

2. In a medium bowl, whisk together the eggs and sugar until just combined. Whisk in the honey and salt. Add the flour mixture and whisk until just combined. Add half of the melted butter and the orange blossom water and whisk until combined. Then add the remaining butter and whisk again. The batter should be thick but drizzle-able. Press plastic wrap directly on the surface of the batter and refrigerate for at least 4 hours but preferably overnight.

3. When ready to bake the madeleines, set a rack in the middle of the oven and preheat to 425°F / 220°C. Butter two 12-cavity madeleine pans with 3-inch / 7.5cm molds and then dust them with flour, tapping out any excess.

4. Remove the batter from the refrigerator and briefly beat it with a rubber spatula until creamy again. Transfer the mixture to a piping bag and cut the end so it has a ½-inch / 13mm diameter opening. Pipe the batter into the prepared madeleine molds until they are three-quarters full, so they don't overflow in the oven. Put the pans in the refrigerator to chill for 10 minutes.

5. Remove the pans from the refrigerator and bake for 4 minutes, then reduce the oven temperature, without opening the oven door, to 375°F / 190°C and bake until the madeleines are lightly golden on top and the dome springs back when lightly pressed, about 5 minutes.

6. Let the madeleines cool briefly in the pans on a wire rack, then flip them upside down and remove the pan. Flip the madeleines so they are right-side up to make sure the domes aren't deflated. Serve warm. Madeleines are best enjoyed right out of the oven or the day they're baked, but they keep in an airtight container in the refrigerator for 1 to 2 days.

CHOUX

MAKES 24 TO 30 CHOUX

The inspiration for these choux comes from the Dunes Blanches bakery in Bordeaux, where I grew up. Even though they are slightly different, I still feel like I'm back at home every time I pop one in my mouth, which happens at least twice a day. Choux are traditionally filled with crème pâtissière, but I find that a bit heavy, so I fill mine with whipped cream or the chocolate mousse I use in my Chocolate Mousse Cake (page 135; make half the recipe to use here). If you're a real chocolate lover, take it one step further and make chocolate choux by adding 3 tablespoons of unsweetened Dutch-process cocoa powder to the flour.

1 stick / 113g unsalted butter, cut into small pieces
½ cup / 120ml whole milk
1 teaspoon granulated sugar
¾ teaspoon fine sea salt
1 cup / 140g all-purpose flour
3 large eggs
Pearl sugar, for sprinkling
4 cups / 400g Vanilla Bean Whipped Cream (recipe follows)
Powdered sugar, for dusting

1. In a medium saucepan, combine the butter, milk, granulated sugar, salt, and ½ cup / 120ml water. Warm the mixture over medium heat, whisking occasionally, until the milk is simmering, and the butter is melted. Add the flour all at once and stir with a rubber spatula until the flour is fully incorporated and a dough forms. Continue stirring, pressing the dough against the bottom and sides of the pan, until the dough forms a ball and comes back together if you run a spoon through it, about 3 minutes. As the dough cooks, a thin film will form on the bottom of the pan. Remove from the heat and let the dough cool for 5 minutes.

2. Transfer the dough to a stand mixer fitted with the paddle and beat on medium speed for about 1 minute to further cool the mixture. Add the eggs, one at a time, and beat, scraping the bottom and sides of the bowl before each addition and again at the end, until fully incorporated. The dough may appear curdled when adding the eggs, but don't panic—it will come back together once it's fully mixed. Continue beating until the dough is shiny, thick, and smooth, about 30 seconds. Remove the paddle from the stand mixer and use it to scoop up some of the dough, letting it fall back into the bowl. It should form a triangle or "V" shape when it's ready.

3. If baking the choux right away, transfer the dough to a piping bag and use scissors to cut the tip of the bag so the opening has a 1-inch / 2.5cm diameter. If not, the dough keeps in an airtight container in the refrigerator for up to 2 days.

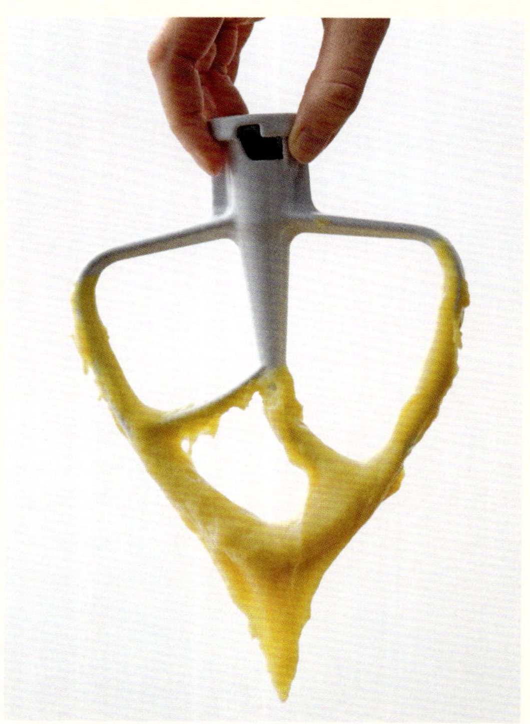

4. When ready to bake the choux, set racks in the upper and lower thirds of the oven and preheat to 400°F / 200°C. Line two 13 × 18-inch / 33 × 45cm or similarly sized baking sheets with parchment paper.

5. Pipe the choux into roughly 2-inch / 5cm rounds onto the prepared baking sheets, leaving about 2 inches / 5cm in between. Use a damp pastry brush to smooth out any "peaks" from piping the choux, then sprinkle them with pearl sugar. Bake for 10 minutes, then lower the oven temperature to 350°F / 180°C. Continue to bake until the choux are golden and look dry on the surface, 8 to 10 more minutes. If you see any shine or moisture on the choux, they may collapse when cooling; continue baking until they look completely dry.

6. Set the pans on wire racks and let the choux cool briefly until they are firm enough to hold their shape. Set the choux directly on the rack to cool completely. Baked (unfilled) choux keep in an airtight container at room temperature for up to 1 day.

7. When ready to serve, fill a piping bag fitted with a plain round tip with ¼-inch / 6mm or similar diameter with the whipped cream. Use a similarly sized or slightly larger open star pastry tip to poke a hole in the bottom of each choux to create space for the whipped cream.

8. Hold a choux lightly in your nondominant hand and use your dominant hand to hold the piping bag. Gently press the pastry tip into the hole in the bottom of the choux, then gently squeeze the piping bag to fill the choux with whipped cream. When you feel light pressure on the choux, it's filled to capacity. Dust the filled choux with powdered sugar and serve! Filled choux are best the day they're filled, but they keep in an airtight container in the refrigerator for up to 1 day.

Vanilla Bean Whipped Cream

MAKES ABOUT 4 CUPS / 400G

Lightly sweetened and flavored with a touch of vanilla bean paste, this classic whipped cream is versatile enough to be used with just about any cake or dessert. This recipe can be easily doubled, tripled, or cut in half—just keep in mind that every 1 cup / 240ml of heavy cream makes about 2 cups / 200g of whipped cream. If you happen to be making a smaller amount—maybe to top hot chocolate (Chocolat Chaud on page 241)—it may be easier to whisk the cream by hand.

2 cups / 480ml heavy cream, cold
4 teaspoons powdered sugar, sifted
2 teaspoons vanilla bean paste

In a stand mixer fitted with the whisk, add the heavy cream, powdered sugar, and vanilla bean paste and whip on medium-high speed for 3 minutes. Increase the speed to high and whip until stiff peaks form, 2 to 3 minutes.

How to

MAKE WHIPPED CREAM

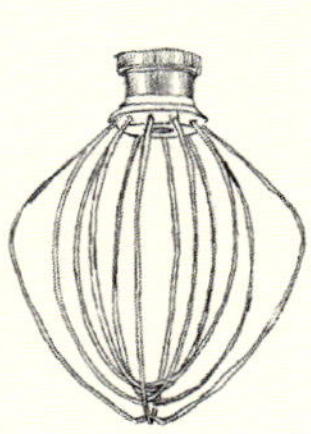

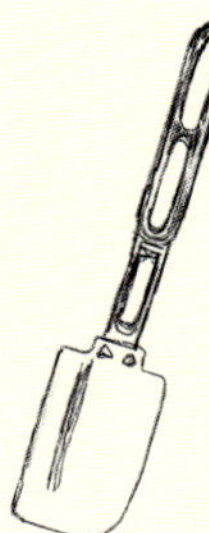

Whipped cream is one of my favorite toppings to make when guests come over—it's light, not overly sweet, and a great alternative to buttercream. It's such an easy and delicious way to finish off desserts, adding the perfect touch of texture and flavor, and you need only a few ingredients. But it's also pretty delicate and can change depending on the temperature outside and in your kitchen, how long you whip it, or how long you need it to last. Here's how I make mine just right—most of the time. Ha!

START WITH THE RIGHT CREAM

Heavy cream and heavy whipping cream are essentially the same. They both contain at least 36% milk fat, which makes thick, stiff whipped cream that's able to hold its shape for longer. Whipping cream, on the other hand, contains 30% to 36% milk fat and that slightly lower fat content means your whipped cream will be slightly less thick and not as stable. I recommend seeking out a high-quality heavy cream (or heavy whipping cream), especially when you're putting the whipped cream between cake layers—it's less important when you're adding a dollop to hot chocolate. Some cartons even list the percentage of milk fat, so you can look for one that contains more milk fat and will therefore whip into a thicker, stiffer, more stable whipped cream.

USE COLD EQUIPMENT AND COLD CREAM

Before you whip your cream, chill your stand mixer bowl and whisk attachment (or your bowl and whisk, if whisking by hand) in the freezer for 30 minutes. Always use fridge-cold heavy cream, which whips more easily.

MAKE SURE YOU GET TO STIFF PEAKS

While it's essential to use higher speeds to whip the most air into your cream and achieve stiff peaks, you also don't want cream splattering out of the mixer! Start by whipping the cream mixture on medium-high speed for 3 minutes, then increase the speed to high and whip for 2 to 3 more minutes until it reaches stiff peaks.

WHIP A MORE STABLE WHIPPED CREAM

If it's warm outside or you want your whipped cream to last a few hours, I recommend whipping it a touch further than usual, to the point that it looks almost curdled. You'll get the same whipped cream experience, but you'll find it holds up better. Another trick is to add a touch of cream of tartar—use ½ teaspoon for every 1 cup / 240ml of heavy cream.

If for some reason you make whipped cream the day before (which I don't recommend), or you find it to be slightly softer than usual, you can bring it back to life by adding a bit of cold, fresh heavy cream (use ¼ cup / 60ml of new heavy cream for every 1 cup / 240ml of original heavy cream) and whipping it again on medium-high speed until stiff peaks form.

BANANA BREAD

MAKES ONE 9 × 5 × 3-INCH / 23 × 13 × 7.5CM LOAF

While I often try to put a twist on classic recipes, when it comes to banana bread, I believe it should stay simple and timeless. With ripe bananas and good butter, this loaf is perfectly moist. You'll notice that the butter quantity is a little wild for such a simple recipe, but I'm very strict about using this exact amount to get an airy loaf with lots of height. If you want to fancy it up, warm a slice and add one of my infused butters (see How to Infuse Butter, page 39).

Canola oil spray or canola oil, for the pan
4 very ripe medium bananas
1¾ cups / 245g all-purpose flour
1¼ teaspoons baking soda
1 teaspoon fine sea salt
1 stick plus 3 tablespoons / 143g unsalted butter, at room temperature and cut into small pieces
1⅓ cups / 265g sugar
3 large eggs, at room temperature
2 teaspoons vanilla extract
⅔ cup / 160g sour cream, at room temperature

1. Set a rack in the middle of the oven and preheat to 300°F / 150°C. Spray or brush a 9 × 5 × 3-inch / 23 × 13 × 7.5cm loaf pan with canola oil.

2. In a medium bowl, use your hands, a potato masher, or a fork to mash the bananas, making sure there are some small chunks remaining.

3. Sift the flour and baking soda into a medium bowl. Add the salt.

4. In a stand mixer fitted with the paddle, beat the butter and sugar on medium speed until fluffy, about 4 minutes. Increase the speed to high and beat for 30 seconds more. Scrape down the bottom and sides of the bowl, then add the eggs, one at a time, and beat on medium-low speed, scraping the bowl before each addition and again at the end, until fully incorporated. Beat in the vanilla.

5. Add the flour mixture in two batches and mix on low speed, scraping the bowl before each addition, just until there are no streaks. Do not overmix! Add the sour cream and mix on low speed just until incorporated.

6. Remove the bowl from the stand mixer, then gently fold in the bananas with a rubber spatula until just incorporated.

7. Scrape the batter into the prepared pan, smoothing the top. Bake until there is a crack on top of the loaf and the center springs back when lightly pressed, about 1 hour. A skewer inserted in the center of the loaf should come out clean (unless you hit a banana—if so, test in a second spot).

8. Let the loaf cool in the pan on a wire rack for 30 minutes. Run a small offset spatula between the edges of the pan and the banana bread, then remove the banana bread from the pan and let cool completely on the rack. If not eating the banana bread right away, cover with a tea towel and leave at room temperature until the next day. The banana bread keeps in an airtight container in the refrigerator for up to 3 days.

RASPBERRY NOUGATINE COOKIES

MAKES 20 TO 24 COOKIES

In France, even the most basic supermarket cookies are often made with chocolate chips and nougatine. Nougatine might seem simple, but it adds so much depth to the flavor of these cookies. It wasn't until I started eating cookies here in the US that I truly appreciated how nougatine enhances chocolate. For this recipe, I use a combination of milk chocolate and raspberry chocolate, which adds a fruity twist that complements the hazelnuts. If you have the opportunity, I highly recommend using Valrhona raspberry fèves—they bake beautifully and deliver that perfect melted chocolate texture you want in every bite.

NOUGATINE

- Canola oil spray or canola oil, for the baking sheet
- ½ cup plus 2 tablespoons / 125g granulated sugar
- 2 teaspoons distilled white vinegar
- ¼ cup / 45g roasted almonds
- ¼ cup / 35g skinless hazelnuts

COOKIES

- 3 sticks / 339g unsalted butter
- 3¼ cups / 455g all-purpose flour
- ¾ teaspoon baking soda
- 1½ teaspoons fine sea salt
- 1½ cups / 300g granulated sugar
- 2¼ cups / 450g (packed) light brown sugar
- 3 large eggs, at room temperature
- 2 teaspoons vanilla extract
- 5¼ ounces / 150g milk chocolate fèves or large chips
- 5¼ ounces / 150g raspberry chocolate fèves or large chips
- Maldon sea salt (optional), for sprinkling

1. FOR THE NOUGATINE: Lightly spray or brush a 9 × 13-inch / 23 × 33cm or similarly sized baking sheet with canola oil.

2. In a wide saucepan, combine the granulated sugar, vinegar, and ¼ cup / 60ml water and stir until combined. Set the pan over medium-high heat and warm, without stirring, until bubbling. Continue to caramelize. As the caramel starts to develop color, carefully whisk it occasionally to even out the caramelization and color. Let it bubble until the caramel is evenly golden, 8 to 15 minutes total, depending on your stove.

3. Remove from the heat, then add the almonds and hazelnuts and stir with a rubber spatula until the nuts are completely coated in caramel. Carefully pour the hot caramel onto the prepared pan and use the rubber spatula to spread it into a thin, even layer, making sure the nuts are fully incorporated into the caramel and not clumped in the middle. Let cool until firm, at least 30 minutes.

4. Once the nougatine is cool, use a metal spatula to remove it from the pan. Transfer it to a food processor and pulse a few times until it's in chunks slightly smaller than ¼ inch / 6mm. (Alternatively, use a knife to chop it by hand.) If you end up with a lot of nougatine "dust," sift the nougatine in a fine-mesh sieve to remove the dust.

5. The nougatine keeps in an airtight container at room temperature for up to 7 days.

6. FOR THE COOKIES: In a medium saucepan, melt the butter over medium-low heat. Remove from the heat and let cool slightly.

7. Sift the flour and baking soda into a medium bowl. Add the fine salt.

8. In a stand mixer fitted with the paddle, beat both sugars on low speed for about 30 seconds to combine. Add the melted butter and beat on medium-low speed until silky and sticky, about 30 seconds. Add the eggs, one at a time, and beat on medium speed, scraping down the bottom and sides of the bowl before each addition and again at the end, until fully incorporated. Add the vanilla and beat, scraping the bowl as needed, until pale and fluffy, about 3 minutes.

9. Add the flour mixture in three batches and mix on low speed, scraping the bowl before each addition, just until there are no streaks. Do not overmix! Add both chocolates and the chopped nougatine and mix until just incorporated.

10. Remove the bowl from the stand mixer. Place a piece of plastic wrap directly onto the surface of the dough, then refrigerate for about 1 hour.

11. Line a pan or a flat-bottomed container that fits in your freezer with parchment paper. Using a large ice cream scoop with a 2-inch / 5cm or similar diameter, scoop the dough into large balls and place the balls, in a single layer, on the lined pan. Wrap the pan or container in plastic wrap and freeze for 30 minutes to 1 hour before baking. (Once the balls are frozen, they can be stored in a resealable freezer bag and kept in the freezer for up to 1 month; bake them straight from frozen.)

12. When ready to bake, set a rack in the middle of the oven and preheat to 350°F / 180°C. Line a 13 × 18-inch / 33 × 45cm or similarly sized baking sheet with a silicone baking mat or parchment paper.

13. Arrange 3 balls of frozen dough on the prepared pan, allowing plenty of room for spreading, then sprinkle generously with the Maldon salt, if using. Bake for about 8 minutes, then rotate the pan and bake until the cookies are crunchy around the edges but still soft in the middle, about 8 minutes more.

14. Let the cookies cool for about 15 minutes on the baking sheet on a wire rack. Use a metal spatula to transfer the cookies to the rack. Enjoy right away or let cool completely. Repeat to bake as many cookies as you like. The cookies keep in an airtight container at room temperature for up to 3 days, or can be well wrapped and frozen for up to 2 months.

BLACKBERRY MUESLI BARS

MAKES 12 BARS

This recipe was born during the peak of the pandemic, in the basement kitchen of my husband, Gurpreet's, Lower East Side cafe, Sunday to Sunday. Back then, people were looking for small comforts—something simple yet uplifting to start their day—and these muesli bars became a morning favorite. They're a perfect balance of fruit and muesli, which I think of as the European cousin of granola—hearty and satisfying but not overly sweet. This recipe is also very flexible. You can use frozen raspberries, blueberries, or black currants for the filling; even a good jam works beautifully.

BLACKBERRY FILLING

1½ pounds / 680g frozen blackberries (about 6 cups), thawed
½ cup / 100g granulated sugar
2 tablespoons all-purpose flour
2 tablespoons freshly squeezed lemon juice (from 1 medium lemon)
1 tablespoon cornstarch

MUESLI

Softened unsalted butter, for the pan
2½ cups / 250g rolled oats
2½ cups / 350g all-purpose flour
1¾ cups / 350g (packed) light brown sugar
1 teaspoon baking powder
½ teaspoon fine sea salt
3 sticks / 339g unsalted butter, melted
1 tablespoon maple syrup

1. FOR THE BLACKBERRY FILLING: In a stand mixer fitted with the paddle, beat the blackberries, granulated sugar, flour, lemon juice, and cornstarch on medium-low speed until combined, about 1 minute. Transfer the filling to a bowl, then clean the stand mixer and the paddle attachment.

2. FOR THE MUESLI: Set a rack in the middle of the oven and preheat to 350°F / 180°C. Lightly butter the bottom and sides of an 8-inch / 20cm square metal baking pan, then line the pan with parchment paper, leaving about 1 inch / 2.5cm hanging over the sides.

3. In a stand mixer fitted with the paddle, mix together the oats, flour, brown sugar, baking powder, salt, and melted butter on low speed until crumbles form, about 30 seconds. Scrape down the bottom and sides of the bowl, then add the maple syrup and mix until it's fully incorporated and the mixture looks like thick wet sand, about 30 seconds.

4. Press about two-thirds of the muesli mixture into the bottom of the prepared pan to create an even base. Bake until lightly golden on the edges, about 15 minutes.

5. Spread the blackberry filling in an even layer to completely cover the baked muesli layer, then sprinkle the remaining muesli evenly over the top—it should completely cover it. Bake until the muesli topping is firm and golden brown, about 30 minutes.

6. Let the bars cool completely in the pan on a wire rack. Carefully wiggle the parchment paper to release the bars from the pan, then lift the parchment and use it to place the bars on a cutting board. Cut into equal squares for serving. The bars keep in an airtight container in the refrigerator for up to 1 week.

SAVORY SCONES

MAKES 16 SCONES

These scones are the only savory item we offer at the bakery, and they've become a favorite among our early risers. The combination of briny olives, tangy sun-dried tomatoes, creamy feta, and fresh chives creates a perfect balance of flavors that's both comforting and satisfying.

One of the secrets to getting these scones light and airy is using floured hands instead of a rolling pin to gently shape the dough. This avoids pressing the dough too tightly, allowing it to rise beautifully when baked. The result is a tender, flaky scone that's ideal for a morning pick-me-up or an afternoon snack. I like to press edible flowers, such as chamomile, into the scones before baking—it's a simple touch that adds unique flavor and a fun final touch. Be sure to handle the dough with care, and you'll have a batch of scones that's just as beloved as the ones we serve at the bakery.

3½ cups / 490g all-purpose flour
3 tablespoons plus 2 teaspoons baking powder
2 tablespoons sugar
2 teaspoons fine sea salt
2 sticks / 227g unsalted butter, cold and cut into small pieces
1 cup / 100g drained finely chopped oil-packed sun-dried tomatoes
⅔ cup / 80g crumbled feta cheese
⅓ cup / 45g chopped pitted green olives
1 teaspoon finely chopped fresh chives
1½ cups / 360g sour cream, at room temperature
2 tablespoons heavy cream
2 large eggs, at room temperature
1 large egg white, at room temperature
Toasted pumpkin seeds and small edible chamomile flowers, for decorating

1. Sift the flour, baking powder, and sugar into a large bowl. Add the salt and cold butter and use your fingers to work the butter into the flour mixture until it resembles coarse crumbs. Add the sun-dried tomatoes, feta, olives, and chives and toss lightly to incorporate.

2. In a medium bowl, whisk together the sour cream, heavy cream, and whole eggs. Add to the flour mixture and mix with a rubber spatula until just incorporated.

3. Tip the dough out onto a lightly floured surface and use floured hands to gently pat it into a round disc about 2 inches / 5cm thick. Dip a 2½-inch / 6cm round metal pastry cutter in flour, then press it firmly into the dough and quickly pull it straight upward. Repeat to cut as many scones as possible, then gently roll or pat the remaining dough into a round roughly 2 inches / 5cm thick and cut more scones. You should have about 16 scones.

4. Line a pan or a flat-bottomed container that fits in your freezer with parchment paper. Arrange the scones, in a single layer, on the lined pan. Wrap the pan or container in plastic wrap and freeze for at least 1 hour before baking. (Once the scones are frozen, they can be stored in a resealable freezer bag and kept in the freezer for up to 3 weeks; bake straight from frozen.)

5. When ready to bake the scones, set a rack in the middle of the oven and preheat to 350°F / 180°C. Line one or two 13 × 18-inch / 33 × 45cm or similarly sized baking sheets with parchment paper.

6. Arrange up to 6 scones on each prepared baking sheet. Brush the tops of the scones with the egg white. Sprinkle the tops with the pumpkin seeds, then press the flowers into the scones. Bake until the scones are golden on both the tops and the bottoms, about 30 minutes.

7. Let the scones cool briefly on the baking sheet on a wire rack. Repeat to bake as many scones as you like. Serve warm or at room temperature. The scones are best the day they're baked, but they keep in an airtight container at room temperature for up to 1 day.

VEGAN PUMPKIN SPICE LOAF

MAKES ONE 9 × 5 × 3-INCH / 23 × 13 × 7.5CM LOAF

I'd never eaten a pumpkin dessert until I moved to the US and discovered how much Americans love anything pumpkin-flavored the second it gets a touch cold outside. I started making this loaf for my vegan customers, and even the nonvegans come back for it! Pumpkin makes this loaf extra moist and flavorful. This is my book agent Leigh's favorite recipe of mine, and it's helped me understand the craze for pumpkin!

PUMPKIN SPICE LOAF

Canola oil spray or canola oil, for the pan
3 tablespoons boiling water
1 tablespoon flaxseeds, finely ground
2 cups / 280g all-purpose flour
2 teaspoons ground cinnamon
1 teaspoon baking soda
1 teaspoon baking powder
½ teaspoon freshly grated nutmeg
½ teaspoon ground ginger
¼ teaspoon ground cloves
½ teaspoon fine sea salt
½ cup / 100g granulated sugar
1 cup / 200g (packed) light brown sugar
1½ cups / 345g canned pure pumpkin puree (not pumpkin pie mix)
¼ cup / 60ml canola oil
1 tablespoon apple cider vinegar
1 teaspoon vanilla extract

CINNAMON GLAZE

3 cups / 360g powdered sugar, plus more as needed
1 teaspoon ground cinnamon
¼ cup / 60ml soy milk
½ teaspoon apple cider vinegar
Pumpkin seeds and small edible flowers (see page 88), for decorating

1. FOR THE PUMPKIN SPICE LOAF: Set a rack in the middle of the oven and preheat to 300°F / 150°C. Spray or brush a 9 × 5 × 3-inch / 23 × 13 × 7.5cm loaf pan with canola oil.

2. In a small bowl, combine the boiling water and ground flaxseeds and let stand for 5 to 7 minutes to create a gelatinous flax "egg."

3. Sift the flour, cinnamon, baking soda, baking powder, nutmeg, ginger, and cloves into a large bowl. Add the salt.

4. In a stand mixer fitted with the paddle, beat the sugars, pumpkin puree, canola oil, and vinegar on low speed, scraping down the bottom and sides of the bowl as needed, until fully combined, about 1 minute. Scrape the bowl, then beat on medium-high speed until creamy, about 30 seconds. Scrape the bowl, then add the flax "egg" and the vanilla and beat on medium speed until fully incorporated, about 1 minute. Scrape the bowl, then add the flour mixture in three batches and mix on low speed, scraping the bowl before each addition, just until there are no streaks. Scrape the bowl again, then beat on high speed for 15 seconds more. Do not overmix!

5. Scrape the batter into the prepared pan, smoothing the top. Bake until a skewer inserted in the center of the loaf comes out clean, about 1 hour.

6. Set the pan on a wire rack set inside a baking sheet and let the loaf cool for 30 minutes. Run a small offset spatula between the edges of the pan and the loaf, then remove the loaf from the pan, place it on the rack, and let cool completely.

7. FOR THE CINNAMON GLAZE: Sift the powdered sugar and cinnamon into the bowl of a stand mixer. Add the soy milk and vinegar and whip on medium-low speed, scraping the bowl as needed, until fully combined, thick, and opaque—it should be the consistency of royal icing—about 1 minute. If the glaze seems too runny, let it stand for a few minutes to firm up. If it's still runny, gradually add more powdered sugar, 1 tablespoon at a time, until you achieve the desired consistency.

8. Slowly pour the glaze over the cooled loaf, still on the wire rack set inside the baking sheet, using a small offset spatula or spoon to push the glaze to completely cover the top and drip down the sides. Before the glaze sets, sprinkle the top with the pumpkin seeds, then press the flowers or petals into the loaf. The loaf keeps in an airtight container at room temperature for up to 3 days.

GINGERBREAD COOKIES

MAKES ABOUT 50 SMALL COOKIES

This recipe is an ode to my grandparents' Swedish neighbor, Margareta, whom I always called my grand-mère de coeur. Margareta was iconic for so many reasons: She always indulged me with whatever I wanted, had impeccable outfits and flawless hair, tore pages out of books after reading them, and most memorably, made the absolute best holiday gingerbread cookies. Every Christmas, we baked her signature cookies and ate most of them, but we also hung them on the tree like ornaments—just as you would with candy canes. The cookies should be soft in the center, snappy on the outside, and perfectly spiced. They're lovely on their own, but I love decorating them with royal icing!

GINGERBREAD COOKIES

1¼ cups / 250g granulated sugar
3½ tablespoons / 75g dark corn syrup
1 stick plus 6 tablespoons / 198g unsalted butter, at room temperature and cut into small pieces
1 tablespoon grated orange zest (from 1 medium orange)
2 tablespoons ground cinnamon
2 teaspoons ground cardamom
1½ teaspoons ground ginger
1½ teaspoons ground cloves
4¼ cups / 595g all-purpose flour
2 teaspoons baking soda

ROYAL ICING

Distilled white vinegar
2 large egg whites, at room temperature
½ teaspoon cream of tartar
4¼ cups / 510g powdered sugar, sifted
1 teaspoon vanilla extract

1. FOR THE GINGERBREAD COOKIES: In a small saucepan, combine the granulated sugar, corn syrup, and ½ cup / 120ml water and bring to a boil over medium heat. Remove from the heat.

2. In a large bowl, combine the butter, orange zest, cinnamon, cardamom, ginger, and cloves. Add the hot sugar mixture and whisk until the butter is melted. Let cool slightly, then add the flour and baking soda and use your hands to gently knead the mixture in the bowl until it forms a smooth dough. Don't overwork it! Wrap the dough in plastic wrap and refrigerate overnight.

3. When ready to bake, set a rack in the middle of the oven and preheat to 400°F / 200°C. Line two 13 × 18-inch / 33 × 45cm or similarly sized baking sheets with silicone mats or parchment paper.

4. On a lightly floured surface, use a floured rolling pin to roll a small portion of the dough into a thin, even layer about ⅛ inch / 3mm thick. Use your favorite cookie cutters to cut the dough into shapes. Arrange the cookies on the prepared baking sheets.

5. Bake until evenly browned, 5 to 8 minutes, rotating about halfway through. Bake them for less time if you prefer softer cookies and longer if you like cookies with more snap.

6. FOR THE ROYAL ICING: Use a paper towel and about ¼ teaspoon of white vinegar to wipe all over the surface of the bowl of a stand mixer, making sure there aren't any traces of liquid or fat.

7. In the clean bowl of a stand mixer fitted with the whisk, add the egg whites and cream of tartar and whip on low speed until foamy. Add the powdered sugar in two batches and whip until combined, then increase the speed to medium-high and whip until thick and glossy with stiff peaks, 7 to 10 minutes. Add the vanilla and briefly whip on medium-low speed to incorporate. (If not using the royal icing right away, press a piece of plastic wrap directly on the surface and keep at room temperature for up to 2 days or in the refrigerator for up to 2 weeks. If the royal icing gets too stiff, gradually whisk in some water, ¼ teaspoon at a time, to loosen it up.)

8. To decorate cookies with royal icing, you'll need a piping bag. For most designs, I prefer using tipless piping bags. They're versatile and easy to work with, and you can customize the size of the opening by cutting the tip—make a very small cut to pipe lines or outlines.

9. When piping, apply steady, even pressure to the bag. Instead of keeping the tip right against the cookie, lift it slightly to let the icing flow naturally onto the surface, creating soft, smooth lines.

10. Start by outlining the cookies. Once the outline is dry to the touch, you can add additional layers or details.

11. Allow the cookies to dry completely at room temperature, uncovered, for at least 12 hours before handling. Once dry, you can stack and store them in an airtight container at room temperature. The cookies keep in an airtight container at room temperature for up to 1 week.

CHOCOLAT CHAUD

SERVES 2

Inspired by my French roots, this hot chocolate draws from the classic chocolat Viennois, a style that is more like a thick, indulgent chocolate sauce than the lighter milk-based versions you might be used to. The key to making it truly exceptional is using the very best chocolate for your ganache. You'll notice the difference immediately when you choose a rich, high-quality chocolate. If you make the ganache ahead of time, store it in the fridge. When you're ready to use it, simply warm it gently in a simmering hot water bath, so the chocolate stays silky and smooth without cooking. I like to top my hot chocolate with a generous swirl of Vanilla Bean Whipped Cream (page 221) or, for an extra touch of sweetness and texture, one of my Meringue Letters (page 71).

1 cup / 240ml whole milk

6 tablespoons / 100g Chocolate Ganache (recipe follows)

1 cup / 100g Vanilla Bean Whipped Cream (optional; page 221)

1. In a small saucepan, warm the milk and chocolate ganache over low heat, stirring until the ganache is fully incorporated into the milk and just until steam starts to rise from the surface; do not let it come to a simmer or bubble.

2. Pour the hot chocolate into mugs, add a big dollop of the whipped cream, if desired, and enjoy!

Chocolate Ganache

MAKES ABOUT 2 CUPS / 475G

8¼ ounces / 235g dark chocolate, preferably 64% cacao, chopped
1 cup plus 1 tablespoon / 255ml heavy cream
¾ teaspoon Maldon sea salt

1. Add the chocolate to a large heatproof bowl.

2. In a medium saucepan, warm the heavy cream over low heat just until steam starts to rise from the surface; do not let it come to a simmer or bubble. Immediately pour the warm cream over the chocolate and gently stir with a rubber spatula until combined. The ganache will be smooth and silky. Stir in the Maldon salt. The ganache can be used right away or stored in an airtight container in the refrigerator for up to 2 weeks. If refrigerating, let the ganache come to room temperature before using.

PIMENT D'ESPELETTE MILLIONAIRE'S SHORTBREAD

MAKES 16 BARS

Millionaire's shortbread will always take me back to the time I spent doing my master's at Leeds University in England, where I spent more time at my friends' flat than my own. Every Tuesday, I'd find myself at their place, joining eight medical students to watch *The Great British Bake Off.* With Yorkshire tea in hand, we'd watch together—while I devoured their stash of millionaire's shortbread.

These bars are a nod to those days, but with a little twist that reflects my own culinary roots. The shortbread crust absolutely must be buttery and firm yet tender enough to crumble delicately with every bite. The caramel layer is smooth and salted, adding richness. I like to temper the richness with dark chocolate, letting the caramel and shortbread shine. For a final touch, I mix in a hint of piment d'Espelette. It's a smoky, warm spice traditional in the Pays Basque near my region in France, and it ties everything together beautifully, giving the bars depth and balance. Piment d'Espelette is pretty easy to find, but you can easily replace it with ground Aleppo pepper.

SHORTBREAD

Softened unsalted butter, for the pan
2 sticks / 226g unsalted butter, at room temperature
½ cup plus 2 tablespoons / 125g granulated sugar
2 cups / 280g all-purpose flour
½ teaspoon fine sea salt

CARAMEL

1 (14-ounce / 397g) can sweetened condensed milk
¾ cup plus 2 tablespoons / 175g (packed) light brown sugar
1 stick / 113g unsalted butter, cut into small pieces
¼ cup / 60ml light or dark corn syrup
¼ teaspoon fine sea salt

CHOCOLATE

8 ounces / 225g dark chocolate, preferably 70% cacao, chopped
¼ cup / 60ml heavy cream
1 tablespoon ground piment d'Espelette
Maldon sea salt (optional)

1. FOR THE SHORTBREAD: Set a rack in the middle of the oven and preheat to 350°F / 180°C. Lightly butter the bottom and sides of an 8-inch / 20cm square metal baking pan, then line the pan with parchment paper, leaving about 1 inch / 2.5cm hanging over the sides.

2. In a stand mixer fitted with the paddle, beat the butter and granulated sugar on medium-high speed, scraping down the bottom and sides of the bowl as needed, until light and fluffy, about 2 minutes. Add the flour and fine salt and beat on medium-low speed for about 30 seconds, then increase the speed to medium and beat, scraping the bowl as needed, until the dough comes together, about 2 minutes.

3. Using your hands, press the dough into the prepared pan, spreading it into the corners and creating an even layer. Bake until the edges are lightly golden, about 30 minutes.

4. Let the shortbread cool completely in the pan on a wire rack before adding the caramel.

5. FOR THE CARAMEL: In a medium saucepan, combine the sweetened condensed milk, brown sugar, butter, corn syrup, and fine salt and cook over medium heat, whisking occasionally, until the butter is melted and the ingredients are fully combined. Continue cooking, whisking constantly as the caramel bubbles and slightly darkens in color, until it registers 235°F / 113°C on an instant-read thermometer. The caramel will be thick and start to pull away from the edges of the saucepan—this will take about 7 minutes. Remove from the heat, then carefully pour the caramel over the cooled shortbread, spreading it into an even layer.

6. Let cool at room temperature, then place the pan in the refrigerator for 30 minutes before adding the chocolate.

RECIPE CONTINUES

7. **FOR THE CHOCOLATE:** Fill a medium saucepan with about 1 inch / 2.5cm of water and bring to a simmer over medium-low heat. In a large heatproof bowl, combine the chocolate and heavy cream, then set the bowl over the pan of simmering water, making sure the water does not touch the bottom of the bowl. Warm the chocolate, stirring occasionally, until melted. Remove the bowl from the pan (careful—it will be warm!) and use a clean kitchen towel to carefully wipe any condensation from the bottom of the bowl. Mix in 2½ teaspoons of the piment d'Espelette.

8. Pour the chocolate over the cooled caramel, spreading it into an even layer. Sprinkle with the remaining ½ teaspoon of piment d'Espelette and Maldon salt, if desired, then let stand at room temperature until the chocolate sets.

9. Carefully wiggle the parchment paper to release the bars from the pan, then lift the parchment and use it to place the bars directly on a cutting board. Use a hot water knife (see Cake Cutting Tips, page 55) to cut into equal squares for serving. The shortbread keeps in an airtight container at room temperature for up to 5 days.

MAÏTÉ
se met à table
YZ

MAÏTÉ se met à table

ACKNOWLEDGMENTS

To **Gurpreet,** my better half—there are no words big enough to thank you for sharing your life with me. I wake up every morning grateful to have you by my side. Getting to share this bakery journey with you is one of the greatest joys of my life. I don't say it enough, but From Lucie should really be called From Lucie and Gurpreet. Without you, I'd still be baking one cake a day in our tiny apartment kitchen. Your courage, clarity, and knowledge are a constant source of strength—and qualities I hope to learn from every day. For now, simply living beside you, watching you thrive, and building this business together—alongside our other baby, Sunday to Sunday—is a true blessing. I love this life with you. Thank you for your endless patience while I wrote this book, cried over this book, and baked a thousand walnut cakes (even though you're allergic). Thank you for being the best husband, the best partner, and more than I ever could have dreamed of in a person.

To my **customers** and **followers**—I do this for you. We've been on this journey together from the very beginning. Thank you for making it possible. From backing the Kickstarter that brought From Lucie, the tiniest bakery, to life, to returning religiously for your favorite cookie or slice of cake, sharing stories from your day, trusting me with your weddings and celebrations, or simply following along as I navigate this beautifully chaotic path—every part of it has meant the world to me. It's all thanks to you, and I hope we'll keep sharing our love for sweets for many more years to come.

To **Leigh Eisenman,** my extraordinary book agent, with the biggest sweet tooth—thank you for believing in me even before the bakery existed. Your patience, professionalism, and wise guidance have meant the world to me, but even more than that, thank you for being a true friend throughout this journey. During the moments that felt uncertain or lonely, you were always there to lift me up and remind me that everyone wants cake. I'll never take that for granted. Thank you for steering me in the right direction and giving me the confidence I didn't know I had. And I'm sorry for always being a little late or disorganized—blame it on my French side.

To **Susan Roxborough, Mia Johnson, Stephanie Huntwork, Darian Keels,** and the entire **Clarkson Potter** team—thank you for your unwavering support and belief in me and this project. I'm so grateful for the opportunity to bring this book to life with you. I couldn't have asked for a more thoughtful, talented, and encouraging team to guide me along the way. Thank you for your patience, your flexibility, and for helping shape the design in a way that feels deeply personal to me.

And a special thank you to **Raquel Pelzel** for believing in my vision.

To **Lauren Salkeld,** whose patience deserves an award—thank you for the countless hours you've poured into this book, treating it as if it were your own. I probably would've written down one recipe and called it a day if it weren't for your dedication, your deadline magic, and your constant push to keep me moving forward. Thank you for noticing every detail, for spending hours testing more than half the recipes, and for making this experience feel personal, supportive, and full of warmth. There will always be a slice of cake waiting for you at the bakery.

To **Katy Busam,** the backbone of From Lucie, my friend, my bakery manager, and the queen of making this wild ride look as easy as riding a bike. I'll forever be grateful to you for helping bring this bakery and this dream to where it is today. You give to others before ever thinking of yourself, and you've made From Lucie feel like home, uplifting everyone around you along the way. I couldn't have asked for a better right hand through it all. You helped develop many of these recipes, baked *every* cake, dessert, and pastry for the photoshoot, and somehow did it all with a smile. I never take your hard work for granted. Thank you for pouring your heart, your hands, and your brilliance into making this book possible.

To **Lucia Bell-Epstein,** my dear friend and the most talented photographer. When this book was just an idea, I knew the photos could be taken only by you. Our worlds intertwined in a way that felt fated, and even when we barely knew each other, it felt like we had known each other for years. I'll always cherish our time at my family's home in France, where you stepped into a new place, made it your own, and went above and beyond, capturing not just the planned shots but every morsel of life in between—the little pauses, the quiet magic, and the unspoken moments only an artist like you could see. I'm forever grateful to have created this deeply personal project with you. The pictures *are* the book.

To **Maya Netzer Horton**—my Maya. You have been there from the very beginning, making my first pop-up happen at Alimentari Flâneur back in 2020, and by my side when the bakery first opened its doors in 2023. Your artwork still hangs on the walls, a quiet reminder of your presence and your magic. Your illustrations are pure poetry, reflecting the way you live: with grace, joy, and total bliss. I'm so proud to have your work woven throughout this book, and I wouldn't have wanted anyone else to bring it to life.

To **Rebecca Bartoshesky**—thank you for your endless patience in helping me discover what I love, and for your incredible talent in understanding a visual world I don't even fully understand myself. As a true Libra, making decisions is not exactly my strong suit, but your talent for curation and thoughtful selection of props made everything feel effortless. If I could relive those ten days, with all of us tucked away in that Brooklyn studio, I would do it again and again. And a heartfelt thank you to **Allie Ayers,** whose support and presence made everything run even more smoothly.

To **Pearl Jones**—your energy lights up every room and makes each day feel more joyful, creative, and inspired. Thank you for making those ten long days feel easy, when they could have felt exhausting. You brought a fresh perspective and playfulness exactly when we needed it most. You make food styling look like a piece of cake, and you find beauty in places I might overlook or try to hide. As someone who loves decorating food, I not only learned new tricks from you—I learned a whole new way of seeing it. And for that, I'll always be grateful.

To **Xander Rapparport** and **Layton Davis,** who can spend hours discussing how realistic their lighting looks—and you see throughout the book that it truly is. Thank you, Xander, for being endlessly flexible as we pulled you in every direction. And thank you, Layton, for letting me blast bad French rap while holding your light rig steady on an apple box—or whatever that thing is called.

To **Molly Weisman,** who came to my rescue and tested the final batch of recipes in this book—while pregnant, no less. And for picking right back up with testing only two weeks after giving birth. If that's not real dedication (or a sugar rush in action), I don't know what is. Thank you for always being so enthusiastic about my recipes and for sharing the most honest—and sweetest—feedback from both you and your daughter. I hope others find as much joy in these recipes as you did.

To my **From Lucie team**—none of this would exist without you. Thank you for everything you do. You are the heart and soul of this bakery. All of your joy, dedication, care for our customers, and creativity in developing recipes help this little bakery grow every single day. It truly takes a village, and I'm so grateful this one is ours. A special thank you to **Katie Robinson,** for your long days, your beautiful tiered cakes, and your patience with my ever-repeating playlist and the chaos I tend to bring into the kitchen. To **Cicely Hunscher** and **Taylor Dietrich**—thank you for being endlessly supportive throughout this project. You've been my right hands, my organized brains, and my biggest cheerleaders as I came to you with all my wild ideas. Thank you for making sure everything came to life while still keeping the bakery running smoothly.

To my **parents, Mutts** et **Papa**—I could write a whole book about how much I want to thank you for raising me the way you did and for being my biggest inspiration. You gave me the freedom to find myself, never imposing any version of who you thought I should be. You showed me the beauty in small things—long family meals, creating with your hands, and noticing the quiet magic in everyday life. But most of all, you taught me the value of love: for home, for family, for one another. Thank you for giving me the work ethic I carry with me, and the deep emotional rhythm that lets me feel things before I can name them, the same rhythm that lives in this book, page after page, feeling after feeling.

To my parents-in-law, **Harileen** and **Pritpal,** the first to believe in my wild cake dream. I still remember you sitting in your car during peak COVID, telling me, "If that's what's making you feel alive, do it with all your heart—great things will follow." Thank you for helping bring this bakery to life, for always believing in me, and for offering your wise guidance whenever I had a tough decision to make. You are the kind of family one only dreams of when far from home. You welcomed me with open arms and made New York feel like home—and for that, I'll forever be deeply thankful.

To my **family** and **friends**—thank you for always cheering me on throughout this journey. To my sister, **Margot,** for being there from the very beginning of From Lucie, helping me make sense of my creativity, and always being just a phone call away during the hard moments. To my brothers, **Hugo** and **Pierre,** who remind me not to take life too seriously and who encourage me to keep doing what makes my heart happy. To my cousins, uncles, and aunts—thank you for inspiring me and for helping bring this dream to life in so many ways. To my friends, near and far—thank you for being the first to lift me up. To **Ralph,** thank you for being my first taste tester and harshest critic. A special thank you to **Ashley,** my fellow bakery owner and dear friend—you've helped make this industry feel less daunting and more personal, offering wisdom, support, and friendship every step of the way. It's your fault that I opened the bakery—and I'm so glad you pushed me to do it. You all make me want to keep moving forward and keep feeding you cake, even when you say you're full.

To my dog, **Dalida,** who would happily steal the carrots from any carrot cake. Thank you for bringing me unconditional love in a city and a career, in which that can be hard to come by. After long days of work, you help me disconnect, slow down, and remember why I started this journey in the first place: to live a meaningful life filled with the things I love to do and the people (and pets) I love the most.

To my childhood home, **Carbonneau in France,** and to my new home, **New York**—thank you for building me. Two opposite worlds: one rooted in the beauty and stillness of the countryside, the other alive with the creativity and constant motion of the city. Together, you made me who I am today.

INDEX

T

V

W

Y

Z

CLARKSON POTTER/PUBLISHERS
An imprint of the Crown Publishing Group
A division of Penguin Random House LLC
1745 Broadway
New York, NY 10019
clarksonpotter.com
penguinrandomhouse.com

Library of Congress Cataloging-in-Publication Data
Names: Ferriere, Lucie Franc de, author | Salkeld, Lauren, author | Bell-Epstein, Lucia, photographer | Netzer, Maya, illustrator
Title: Cake from Lucie: recipes and techniques from the French countryside to New York City / Lucie Franc de Ferriere with Lauren Salkeld; photographs by Lucia Bell-Epstein; illustrations by Maya Netzer.
Description: [New York] : [Clarkson Potter], [2026] | Includes index.
Identifiers: LCCN 2025011681 (print) | LCCN 2025011682 (ebook) | ISBN 9780593799758 hardcover | ISBN 9780593799765 ebook
Subjects: LCSH: Cake | Pastry | Cooking, French | From Lucie (Bakery) | LCGFT: Cookbooks
Classification: LCC TX771 .F675 2026 (print) | LCC TX771 (ebook) | DDC 641.86/50944—dc23/eng/20250416
LC record available at https://lccn.loc.gov/2025011681
LC ebook record available at https://lccn.loc.gov/2025011682

ISBN 978-0-593-79975-8
Ebook ISBN 978-0-593-79976-5

Editors: Susan Roxborough and Darian Keels
Editorial assistant: Elaine Hennig
Designer: Mia Johnson
Production designer: Christina Self
Production editor: Liana Faughnan
Production: Kim Tyner
Compositors: Merri Ann Morrell and Zoe Tokushige
Digital tech: Xander Rapparport
Photography 1st Assistant: Layton Davis
Baker: Katy Busam
Color correction and retouching: Vitreous
Baker assistant: Taylor Dietrich
Food stylist: Pearl Jones
Prop stylist: Rebecca Bartoshesky
Prop stylist assistant: Allie Ayers
Copy editor: Kate Slate
Proofreaders: Eldes Tran, Sigi Nacson, Hope Clarke, and Jane Hardick
Indexer: Elizabeth Parson
Publicist: Lauren Chung
Marketer: Andrea Portanova

Manufactured in China

10 9 8 7 6 5 4 3 2 1

First Edition

The authorized representative in the EU for product safety and compliance is Penguin Random House Ireland, Morrison Chambers, 32 Nassau Street, Dublin D02 YH68, Ireland, https://eu-contact.penguin.ie.